The Glass *Is* Full

THE SECRETS TO BEING HAPPY
AND STAYING HAPPY

Gigi G.

The Glass *Is* Full

THE SECRETS TO BEING HAPPY
AND STAYING HAPPY

Gigi G.

BALBOA
PRESS
A DIVISION OF HAY HOUSE

Copyright © 2012 Gigi G. (Jehane I. Ghabrial)

All rights reserved. No part of this book may be used or reproduced by any means, graphic, electronic, or mechanical, including photocopying, recording, taping or by any information storage retrieval system without the written permission of the publisher except in the case of brief quotations embodied in critical articles and reviews.

ISBN: 978-1-4525-5846-2 (sc)
ISBN: 978-1-4525-5847-9 (e)

Library of Congress Control Number: 2012916377

Balboa Press books may be ordered through booksellers or by contacting:

Balboa Press
A Division of Hay House
1663 Liberty Drive
Bloomington, IN 47403
www.balboapress.com
1-(877) 407-4847

Because of the dynamic nature of the Internet, any web addresses or links contained in this book may have changed since publication and may no longer be valid. The views expressed in this work are solely those of the author and do not necessarily reflect the views of the publisher, and the publisher hereby disclaims any responsibility for them.

The author of this book does not dispense medical advice or prescribe the use of any technique as a form of treatment for physical, emotional, or medical problems without the advice of a physician, either directly or indirectly. The intent of the author is only to offer information of a general nature to help you in your quest for emotional and spiritual well-being. In the event you use any of the information in this book for yourself, which is your constitutional right, the author and the publisher assume no responsibility for your actions.

Any people depicted in stock imagery provided by Thinkstock are models, and such images are being used for illustrative purposes only.
Certain stock imagery © Thinkstock.

Printed in the United States of America

Balboa Press rev. date: 10/05/2012

My Inspirations

For my loving husband, Christopher, who has shown me the true meaning of love and encouraged me to be myself. Because of Chris, my journey towards self-love, self-acceptance, and self-fulfilment has been (and is still) the greatest journey of my life. Because of his unconditional acceptance and love—and his belief in me and his encouragement—I have chosen to share the secrets of my journey towards happiness with you. Now you can also enjoy this great journey!

For my parents, Joe and Sonia (Sunny), who have given me every opportunity to express myself and flourish. Especially for my mother, Sunny, my spiritual mentor, who opened my heart to the realms of the universe and the experiences it has to offer.

For my beautiful children, Isabelle and Felicity—my angels, the lights of my life, the completion of my journey of self. You have taught me so much about unconditional love and what it means to be free. Your joy, your love, your energy, your innocence—those things that we grown-ups seem to lose touch with (but need to embrace again in our lives). The key to freedom and success is to be more like you both. I have learned this from both of you. I thank you for being such a large part of my own journey in this life. Love, Mummy xxx

For my very first spiritual healer and guide, Gwen Burghes, who set me on my own journey towards physical and spiritual well-being.

Contents

Preface	xi
Introduction	xvii
Laying the Foundations	1
The Next Step Forward	11
Say "Thank You"	12
Say "Sorry"	15
Is Your Glass Full Yet?	28
Look at the View from the Penthouse, Not the Basement!	35
If You Believe in Life, Life Will Believe in You!	39
Freedom. What Is It?	41
First things first	42
You can choose to feel worthy—it is **your** choice	43
Now Let's Move to the Next Step: Your Feelings about Yourself!	52

Let Go!	**56**
Healing Wounds	58
"The Tree"	**65**
Time out!	**69**
Take Steps Forward *with Courage*	**72**
"Things Don't Matter, People Matter"	**77**
Risky Business	**81**
Every Childhood Has Its Ups and Downs	**85**
Live Life in the Moment! Make the Most of the Now!	**87**
Forgiveness Is a Healing Gift You Give Yourself!	**92**
Change the Label!	**95**
Sweep away the Anger!	**98**
How to express any anger in a healthy and productive way	100
Take Responsibility for Your Existence—Take Charge!	**104**
Goodbye, Guilt!	**106**
You Matter!	**110**
Say "Sayonara" to Shame	**114**
Living Positively	**118**
Letting Go of Desires for Revenge	**124**
Relax!	**127**
Life Is Like a Big Bowl of Soup!	**133**
Smile and the Whole World Will Smile with You	**137**
Be Kind to Yourself and to Others	**140**

Slow Down and Enjoy the Journey	143
Sing Your Way to Freedom	150
The Classical Effect	153
Let the Light in!	159
Life's a Beach!	164
Be True to Yourself—Dare to Follow Your Dreams	167
The Allegory of the Frog: Run Your Own Race	169
Seize Your Opportunities … Now!	172
Be Your Own Best Friend	178
Get up off the Lounge and Live Your Life!	180
Change It Up!	183
Treat Yourself!	185
Get Your Own Endorphins into Gear!	188
Turn down the Heat!	194
Have Faith!	198
Treat Others as You Want Them to Treat You!	203
Every Life Experience Is Positive	206
You Are *Never* Alone!	209
Trust Yourself, Your Inner Guide, and the God within You!	213
Let It Be!	215
Gather Yourself and Pull Your Life Together	218
A Look at Gigi G.	220

Preface

Welcome!

You have chosen to read this book for a reason. There is a reason behind everything that happens in this life. And what an exciting journey it is going to be! Do you know why? Because you are finally going to realise that *you* hold the power to make it an exciting journey.

It will be a journey of becoming empowered and actually feeling that power within you. A journey in which your whole perspective of this life will change in ways that will make you feel better because you will view it in a positive way!

It will be a journey in which the words "I can't" get thrown out the window, and you finally realise and *believe* that there are no limits to what you can do (because you control what you do and how you view this life). You—and you alone—hold that key and that power ... no matter what the situation might be!

It will be a journey in which you discover that every minute of every day you can make the choice to say, "Yes, I can"—and then you can go ahead and do it. Believe me ... it is that easy!

It will be a journey in which you learn and understand that you are a physical, spiritual, and emotional person—and that all three of those parts of you need to coexist and work together to bring about harmony within you.

"So what does *The Glass IS Full* actually mean?" you ask.

Well ... think about it for a minute. Most of us will remember being told when young, "When you see a glass filled halfway with water, see it as a glass half-full, not as a glass half-empty." To an extent, that's true. But thinking of the glass in that way is not realising the full potential of being positive in your life. What do I mean?

Ask yourself, "What things in this world are the most important for our survival?"

One obvious answer is water. Everyone knows we can't survive without water. You learn on all of those survival shows on TV these days that if you get stuck in the middle of nowhere, make sure you stay hydrated. Am I right, or am I right?

But one thing everyone forgets (especially in Western society) is how important air is. We just can't survive without air … can we?

Do you get why the glass is always full now?

When I look at a glass, if it is half-full of water, I not only see the water, but also I see that it is half-full of air. So it is *always* full! Even when the glass appears to have no water in it, it is still full of air. It is *always* full.

How easy life is when you adopt this way of looking at the glass and put it into effect in your life.

For example, everything that happens each minute of your day presents the opportunity for you to learn something. Everything!

Every moment of every day is *full* of experience and life. Even the ability to live, to breathe air, is a gift in itself.

When you view your life as a glass that is always full of something, no matter what happens around you, you will always feel fulfilled. Your life will always feel full and filled. That is the secret to happiness!

I think this has to be the problem with this modern Western society: most people just want more and more and more. They never see their glasses (that is, their lives) as full of happiness. They focus on what's missing! And it's not usually what's missing inside—it's usually what they have on the outside that seems to matter most!

"My house isn't big enough", "My boobs aren't big enough", "I want to wear that designer's clothes because everyone else is", "I want more money", "I want, I want, I want."

In our instant gratification society, people spend too much time worrying about what's on the outside. They use fad diets, pills, cosmetic surgery, and credit cards to fix it their problems, but they forget to live in the moment and feed their soul with those moments. Money can't buy those conscious moments. They forget to stop and listen to the sounds of life and appreciate the fact that they are alive. That in itself is a miracle, but we forget this fact very quickly. If you remember to appreciate every experience and view each day of your life as an experience from which you can grow and learn, you won't feel the need to fill your life with stuff. You will always lead a full life, no matter what you have.

That doesn't mean you can't work hard and earn money to pay your bills. It is just how you view your life that makes it a happier one. If you see your life as full, you will wake each day feeling happy. This has an effect on how you work and perform. That joy for life will translate into your work and your life, and you will always be fulfilled. The money just comes. It is a gift, but it doesn't rule your life. After all, however much money you have, your view of the world will be as follows: "I have everything, and I enjoy everything I have." The universe will keep sending it to you. The minute you start seeing your life as not being fulfilled, you will always see it that way. Negative energy breeds negative energy.

It's time to put those glasses on and see the world through those new lenses. It's time to start appreciating every moment as a gift of sorts. That seems simple enough, doesn't it? Believe me: it is that simple!

All you have to do is believe!

Your Glass *IS* Full.

Introduction

Welcome to your new beginning!

Today, you start your journey on the road of peace, love, joy, and happiness. A journey where your world is a wonderful place filled with a wealth of experiences and growth.

It's your fate that you have picked up this book. There is reason and purpose behind everything that happens to you (and around you) in your life. Sometimes you might not know what that reason or purpose is, but one thing you can always be sure of is that there is a reason or purpose for everything. One day—whether it is now, in a month, or even many years from now—you will realise what that purpose was.

Gigi G.

What you can also be sure of is that the universe knows you have a true need for happiness and success in your life—and that you need some help finding a way to get there. Consider me your guide, and consider that your life is like a big map—the paths in your life are like the roads or routes on that map.

There are so many different routes you can take to get to your destination. And though there might appear to be a dead end on some of the streets, you will always be able to navigate your way there … even if it means taking the long route.

As you begin this journey, it is so important for you to understand a very basic rule: you can't buy happiness or acquire it from others. You can only create it for yourself. It has to come from within you, not from outside of you. There are no exceptions to this rule. So, you have to put aside everything that you have been conditioned to think about happiness. Rather, you must turn to yourself for it.

Each day, when you wake up, remind yourself of this very basic rule.

No matter how out of control you or your life might feel, always remember that you are the one who ultimately controls your own life. You control your own feelings and reactions to situations. You are the one who has complete control over how you view situations.

By remembering these simple rules, you free yourself from the chains of having your feelings dictated by the outside world and those around you.

"Yes," you say, "but what if bad things happen to me that I can't control?"

After many years of being you, you have developed your own ideas of how you and your life should be. You have developed your own ideas about what is good and what you believe to be bad. You react to situations in certain ways because you have your own ideas about what those situations mean to you. Sure, at the end of the day, those things that happen around (and to) you might not always be in your control. But what is in your complete control is *how* you see those situations. And how you see those situations will affect how you feel about them and yourself.

Knowing *you* have complete power to change the way *you* view situations—and complete power to change the way *you* feel about them and react to them—is the key to your success in life.

How?

By *always* seeing the positive in *every* situation, no matter how negative it might seem at first. I guarantee you there is always a positive side to everything—a positive way of viewing things, a benefit that flows from it in one way or another.

Gigi G.

Sometimes the positive is really obvious ... sometimes it isn't.

When the positive is not obvious to you, you need to just say to yourself, "I know the positive is there, I just have to look a little harder for it."

Sometimes you just have to sit down, take out a pen and notepad, and write a list with the word *positive* at the top. And then you just sit there and focus. In no time at all, you will start writing the positive things you can think of. I guarantee you that one of the big positives of every situation is that it is a life experience that you'll learn from. And you won't just learn about that situation, you'll also learn about yourself (and sometimes the people around you). There's a few positives right there! See how easy that was?

When you practise writing lists, you will come to realise there is a lot to be thankful for, regardless of how negative things might appear at first. You will also eventually be able to start making mental lists of the positives. It's all just a matter of practise.

If you focus on doing your written (or mental) lists every day, your brain will end up retraining and rewiring itself to be positive and see the positive in everything. That's how easy it can be! It might come naturally to you, or it might take some work or practise—but either way, you will get there!

"But how does all of this make me happy?" I hear you all ask.

Just think about it. It's actually very simple when you know what the secret is.

When you look at the positive in *everything*, you will never have any reason to feel bad or react badly, will you?

Let me give you an example. Let's start with the phrase, "Money doesn't buy happiness." How true that is!

Sure, money makes life easier to cope with, but only from a financial point of view (paying bills, buying food, and keeping a roof over your head). But that is all outside of you. Money doesn't pay for your reactions. Money doesn't pay for your feelings. How ridiculous would it be if I said to you, "Can I buy your self-love and inner peace for $2,000?" You would laugh at me, wouldn't you? How on Earth are you going to sell me that?

So what makes people think they can buy those things? The short answer is, they just can't.

And what you need to do is put aside everything you have been told about money and start from scratch … with *you!*

Money can never buy self-worth or self-confidence or self-love. If it could, some of the celebrities in this world making millions of dollars wouldn't have problems with alcohol or drugs or moving in and out of relationships, right?

Gigi G.

Before you are able to enjoy the wonderful things and positive experiences your life has to offer, you have to connect with yourself. You have to connect with what is natural and can't be bought: the beauty of nature and the universe. There are so many ways you can do this, and I will challenge your way of thinking and give you techniques to help you change the way you view the world and others. And before you know it, you will see your life in a completely different way. You will have a new appreciation for yourself and life. And with your new tools and outlook on life, your life will change—and happiness will follow.

Just read on with an open mind and open heart. You deserve to give yourself that gift.

And after travelling on this journey with me, the remainder of your life will leap forward in an extremely exciting way. You will find your own special road to freedom and happiness.

Always remember that you are a unique and special person. There is no one else exactly like you out there. You deserve happiness, and together, we will work at getting that for you.

So: "All aboard!" Let your journey begin!

Laying the Foundations

The first building block (foundational stone) to support this monument we call our happy life is the understanding that out of what appears to be adversity comes strength and direction.

Every experience moves us forward to the next experience.

That move forward to the next step can be a great journey when we embrace the lessons learned from previous experiences. No matter what those previous experiences were, they will always provide additional strength for your foundations and direction in your life. Each experience will be just another block that you can add to your foundation—and each will allow you to build your life and establish who you are.

The next building block is to realise and believe that the world actually is a great and amazing place—you just need to be open to it, stay positive, and always keep the faith. This part of the building process is to develop the skill of pushing aside negative thoughts and changing each of those thoughts into a positive one.

Another key to the strength of your foundations is to accept others as they are and to live every moment with gratitude.

My mother, who is always giving me great advice, says, "Accept others as they are, and you will always be happy because you will never be disappointed." Another of my favourites is, "Without expectations, you will never experience disappointment. Just live in the moment and enjoy it for what it is."

Even better is a quote my five-year-old child has been saying (how much we can learn from the simplicity and beauty of a child!): "Get what you get and don't be upset." As simple as that might sound, it is actually a great piece of advice. And this came from my five-year-old child! If you don't have expectations and just accept everything you have in this life, you will never have reason to be upset or disappointed. It is only when you fill your head with expectations of how you think your life should be that disappointment can arise when you don't get what you expect.

As I grew up, my mother also taught me two very important things (which also serve as building blocks for life): "If you don't have anything nice to say, don't say anything at all" and, "If you have something nice to say, say it! But don't just say nice things unless you are sincere. Flattery is not sincere. Never resort to flattery. Sincere appreciation and flattery are two very different things. One comes from the heart, the other from the teeth out."

The next building block is a combination of sincerity, honesty, and kindness in actions and words—when dealing with yourself *and* others.

Avoid using words that radiate negativity; find a way to express what you want to say using positive words. Remember that the glass *is* full. There is always a way to see any situation positively and describe it using positive words.

It's like I said before: sometimes the positive is easy to see, and other times, we just have to look a little harder to find it. Maybe a magnifying glass would do the trick! Increase the size of the picture and look for the positive. The best way to do this is to sit down with a pen and paper and make yourself write down as many positive things about the situation as you can. The more you do this, the more skilled you become at doing it. Eventually, when there is a situation that everyone sees as disastrous, you will see a small glimmer of goodness and hope and positivity in it.

Always remember that everything happens for a reason—even if you don't know what that reason is then and there, even if you don't know what that reason is until much later. When you trust that there is reason in everything that happens and go with the flow (like the foam on the water, moving with the waves in the sea), you won't feel like your life is stuck in a traffic jam. The journey will feel more smooth when you know that—no matter what—your destination is always going to be there waiting for you. After knowing this, you start enjoying the journey there. And before you know it, the journey there becomes the best part. It is from the enjoyment of your journey through life that you will get your happiness.

Another building block of your life is the knowledge that positive, accepting, and gentle communication is an amazing thing. Only greatness can come out of goodness. Miscommunication, misunderstanding, and lack of appreciation for each other's perspectives or points of view can create barriers between each of us. Before making negative assumptions about what the meaning of people's actions are, face them and find out whether your interpretation of their actions is correct. I mean, how silly would it be to waste your energy feeling negatively about someone because of the person actions or words?

Always remember that, although we are all humans, we all act and behave very differently. And we extract the meaning of another's behaviour based on our own interpretation of that person's behaviour. This process of interpretation is usually infected by our own views of the world. We might be completely off base. How do you avoid misinterpretation? One good way is to check with the source of the information you are interpreting. You could be losing the chance to know someone simply because you are too embarrassed or stubborn to find out whether the person means to convey the message you receive.

Having faith that there is goodness in everyone is *the* starting point. Only then can you put yourself in that person's shoes to try to figure out what that person needs to bring the goodness out.

Sometimes, we might not bring out the goodness straight away. This doesn't mean it is useless trying—it just means you haven't quite figured out what that person really needs to bring his or her goodness out. Sometimes it takes a little imagination and research. If we keep trying to reformulate new ways of reaching that person, the goodness will shine out eventually. One day, all the hard work will pay off because that goodness finally shines through.

Always remember that there is good in everyone—and greatness comes from goodness. In this, you can have complete faith.

Sometimes, you just have to keep all of that in mind when things or people seem bad. You must have faith that dealing with things with goodness and a positive heart and mind will eventually produce the greatness we desire—not only from ourselves, but also from those around us.

Another building block is the understanding that you can be your own worst enemy. Self-criticism, self-doubt, and lack of self-acceptance can be soul destroying. And sometimes people can feel stuck in a pattern of self-sabotage and self-destruction.

The minute you understand and realise that you hold the key (the power) to change it all—to rise above it and blossom—you will shed those old ways and move towards happiness.

Another thing you need to know and accept is that there is no such thing as perfection! What you think is perfection—what you think is the ideal—doesn't exist. It is only what you *think* it is, which is based on how you were brought up to see the world (largely materialistically). Sadly, many of us in the capitalistic West have been told that success is measured by what objects we have. But true success in life stems from who we are as people, not what we have.

If you accept and love yourself for who you are—not what you think you should be—and you see the world as a positive and wonderful place, you will be happy with yourself and your life. There can be no greater success than this. Wouldn't you rather have happiness than a life full of stuff (and self-doubt, negativity, and unhappiness)? How could you possibly enjoy your stuff in that sort of state? It defeats the purpose of having the stuff in the first place, doesn't it? You might feel happy for a moment after you get something new, but unless you fix what is inside of you and accept that you are who you are, you won't be happy. Without self-acceptance and self-love, whatever feelings of happiness you have when you get something new will disappear in no time. You will be left with yourself again.

Unless you accept that you are just how you are supposed to be and everything in your life is as it should be, you can never be happy—regardless of what you have or don't have in terms of material goods.

When you strive for something that doesn't exist, such as perfection, you are bound to fail. There is no peak to reach. It is an ever-changing beast because it only exists in your mind and changes with how you feel each day (and how others tell you it should be).

Try this analogy: imagine being the first person in the world to climb a mountain. No one in the world knows whether this mountain has a peak. It just keeps going. People look at the mountain from afar, and the top is always covered in clouds. Everyone assumes that the peak of the mountain is in the clouds. You also think it has a peak because everyone else tells you it does. The more people say it, the more you believe it. You set off and keep going, waiting to get to the top. But you never get there. Slowly, you become discouraged and upset with yourself.

Gigi G.

What's wrong with me? Why haven't I reached the peak yet? you think to yourself. You start to get depressed. You keep striving, but you are never happy because you have not reached the peak yet.

You have spent your whole life climbing to get to this peak, focused on the task ahead of you. You have been moving one step at a time, always looking for the peak through the clouds. One day, you die. All you have been doing is climbing and climbing towards something that never existed in the first place. You have been looking forward, all the time missing out on the amazing view around you and the experiences you could derive from it! That is how many people live their lives.

The trick to living life is not to worry about reaching the peak; otherwise, you miss out on actually living and enjoying your life. Rather, you should enjoy taking each step and remember to take in the view. You should celebrate and congratulate yourself on each step you take. That's the secret to happiness.

Just because others tell you that the peak exists, it doesn't mean it does. The art of living is to forget what others tell you about life and to live each day with joy. You shouldn't worry about where you are going and when you are going to get there.

Don't get me wrong, it is great to have goals in life—things to work towards—just understand that the journey on the way there is the best part. And enjoying the journey there is the most important part. Even if you don't reach the goal, you are still happy because you have enjoyed the experiences working towards it. This is success. This is what happiness is about.

Another building block in the foundations of your life is remembering that loving yourself is the key to all happiness. Once you appreciate all the goodness in yourself and focus on the things you are happy with, you will live and enjoy life with love. Only then can others truly love you in return.

Another key building block in building your foundation is remembering that forgiveness is a great gift you can give yourself. Forgiving yourself for your mistakes is crucial—after all, you are only human (and humans are imperfect).

Forgiving others for their wrongs against you is also important. That forgiveness of others is the greatest gift you can give yourself. When you forgive others, you let go of negative feelings, such as resentment and anger. By forgiving others and yourself, you give yourself the greatest gift of inner peace—the negative feelings that attach to the things you forgive fall away.

This is the ultimate key to happiness: letting go of the negative and being positive.

Gigi G.

The building blocks I have stated, which form the foundations of your new life, are the starting point. They are the tools you need to start building your new life—just like the tools of a builder.

Let's start building!

The Next Step Forward

With your foundations laid, you can move forward. The other tools in this book are techniques to keep you going. They will help you continue building on your foundations.

Just like any structure, when the foundations are laid, the rest of the building can start to take shape.

There are so many ways of living your life in a way that will make it positive. The key is to keep building your life in a positive way with a positive view of the world (and a positive view of everything that happens in it and around you). Always remember the basics: everything is as it should be, everything happens for a reason, and there is always a positive in every situation.

With your foundations in place, the only way is up!

Say "Thank You"

Be thankful for everything in your life—even those experiences you don't view as positive initially. Those challenging experiences will teach you something, and the positivity that flows is the lesson learned.

If you are always thankful for your experiences and everything else in your life, you will always succeed. You will see the results as a positive outcome.

There is always something to be thankful for every day.

Remember to be thankful no matter what appears to be going on in your life at any given moment! This is one of the bricks that will make your "life building" strong. In fact, you should make sure that you have at least one of these *thank you* bricks in each of your storeys as you build your life upward. For each storey you go up, that element is there. The more thankful you are for every moment in life—and for every experience you have—the more positively you will see life. You will have no reason not to be happy.

"But," you say, "what about all the bad stuff that happens to me?"

The first rule is that nothing "bad" happens to you. It is just another experience, from which you can grow and learn. Learning and growing are positive things. In that sense, you already have a positive to this experience you call *bad*.

If, in a moment, things don't feel like they are going the way you had hoped they would (or in a way which would ordinarily make you feel positive), be thankful for something. Change the feeling.

Be thankful that you are alive. Life is a miracle itself. Even if your health may not seem to be the best, you have life! This, in itself, is something to be very thankful for.

By acknowledging the good in every situation, the good multiplies. This happens because your focus is on the good. The key is to focus on the good in every moment of every day in your life. That way, you will always be happy.

Gigi G.

This may sound really simplistic, but it's true. Just think about it for a moment. If you only focus on what is good in your life—even the basic fact that you are alive—you will always have something to make you feel good. It is incredible how this can affect your existence every day.

Saying "thank you" for every moment of every day is an essential building block in your life. With this building block laid, happiness will come because you can only feel happy when you see good in everything. From this happiness will come healing—not just in terms of your health, but also in terms of those emotional and spiritual blocks that have stopped you from seeing life in a positive way. And from that healing will come freedom. And from that freedom will come everything else good that this life has to offer emotionally. And to think it all starts with two very simple words—*thank you*!

Say "Sorry"

Admitting you are not right about something is a great strength. It builds your character. It is another building block on which your most positive life is built.

We are not perfect. Sometimes we get it wrong, and the sooner we recognise this and apologise for it, the sooner we can let go of that negative emotion and keep moving forward in life.

Admitting that sometimes you think in a way that holds you back from being positive is the first step towards doing something about those patterns and thoughts. By recognising that we engage in negative thoughts, we can work each day to face them, challenge them, and grow from them.

"How is knowing I've taken a position that is wrong holding me back?" you ask.

Gigi G.

When you know you are looking at something incorrectly—but you dig your heels in and battle on—all you are doing is entrenching yourself deeper and deeper into a place of wrong. And that is not a positive place to be. It is like digging yourself deeper and deeper into a grave. One day, your hole is so deep that no one (not even yourself) can see you in there—and someone will start filling it with dirt. And then getting out is so much harder!

When you hold on to negative feelings (such as knowing you are adopting a position on something that is not right), and you don't let go of them by saying, "Hey, I'm wrong," you keep digging yourself deeper and deeper into a negative place. Ultimately, your world turns dark, and it is harder to find the way out.

Saying "sorry" is actually about recognising that sometimes you just get it wrong. It allows you to let go of the guilt you hold onto in knowing this fact.

You might think, *Isn't that a negative thing to say?* It depends on how you look at it. It's like checking your car's tyres and recognising that they might need some air put into them. It is the same for you as a person.

There will be moments in your life when you will need to recognise that you might be a little sensitive about things people say or do. You might misinterpret things, and you need to work on being less sensitive so you can see and interpret things with a clear, emotionally unattached mind.

There might be times when you are prone to viewing things in a negative way, and you have to work on viewing things more positively.

There may even be times when you are stubborn about an issue, which means you need to work on recognising there are other ways to approach or deal with the situation.

This is the sort of thing that I mean. It is not a weakness or flaw, per se. It is a recognition that there are times when you will have to work on making the things that hold you back more positive.

How do you do it? Exercise and practise.

When our muscles are weak and small, don't we go to the gym or do some exercise to make them stronger? If you want to build your calf muscles, you ride a bike or do calf lifts (or whatever other exercise focuses on that muscle group to give them strength).

And remember it's not just the workout and exercise you need; it's also allowing time for the muscles to heal before going hard at the next work out. Otherwise, the muscles won't heal properly before the next workout, and you are more likely to damage them. This is what you are like emotionally and spiritually.

Each emotion—each part of your psyche that you need to work on making more positive—is like a muscle that needs to be exercised, rested, exercised, and rested again. Only then can you make it stronger.

Let me give you an example that I bet you have experienced at least once in your life. You had an argument with someone, and you were so stuck in your position—so buried in your point of view—that you simply couldn't move past your position. You ended up having an argument with that person—perhaps your partner or your sibling or your parents or a friend or colleague—and you became so upset and affected by it that you couldn't let go of it. At that point, you couldn't face the person again because of how you felt. Sound familiar?

Being stubborn and not listening to another's perspective (and not accepting that he or she has a right to his or her own point of view) only causes you to create a negative barrier between you and that person. You end up harbouring negative feelings towards that person, and it takes a chunk out of your energy. It just sits inside you, fermenting like milk that is going bad. But you never throw it out!

We've *all* had a moment like this at least once in our lives. You are not alone!

It's time to throw out the bad milk so you can clean yourself out and fill up with some good healthy products. Yes, get rid of those negative feelings by accepting that we all have different points of view because we are all different. How boring it would be if we all thought the same way and were no different from each other. The world would be such a boring and unstimulating place. Be stimulated by other people's points of view. There is no need to change them. And accept your own view as being just that—*your* view. In accepting that others will have different ways of looking at things than you, you don't take on negative energy simply because you hold a different point of view.

The next step is to figure out techniques for getting to the point that you can just allow others to *be*.

Let's start by thinking about some situation in which you found yourself swelling up with anger or other negative emotions because you were arguing with someone who didn't agree with you.

You need to recognise in that situation that there are ways of turning that situation of conflict (that is, the views are conflicting) into a positive situation.

To start things off, grab a pen and some paper. Write down what the argument was about. Now write down what your position was. And then write down what the other person's position was. Now write down the following words:

> I am entitled to have my own view about things.

> Others are just as entitled as I am to have their own views about things.

> I don't have to agree with other people's points of view.

> I don't have to change the views of others to be happy within myself.

I accept that I am different from others and others are different from me. This is what makes the world an interesting place.

> I can learn from others how to see things differently.

Now we are part of the way there! By writing these little reminders, you are starting to implant them into your mind. The more you read them each day, the more implanted they become. Eventually, you won't need to read them anymore. They are just your way of reminding yourself that there is no such thing as right or wrong. Everyone sees the world in a different way, and you can learn different ways of viewing different situations. You don't have to adopt them; all you need to do is accept that there are different perspectives.

Think about it: the reason people argue with each other is because they are trying to change each other's point of view.

But why?

Why is it so important for others to have exactly the same view of the situation as we do?

Have you ever heard the idea that you should just *agree to disagree*? That is the first step you should take when a conflict arises.

Remind yourself that *this person is entitled to his or her own view—just as I am*. And then remind yourself that *there is no need to force others to have the same view that I have*.

Just listen to them, and you will actually learn something. You will learn another way of looking at the same situation that you have your own view about.

Remind yourself that there is no right or wrong—just different perspectives.

Try to understand where that person is coming from—from where that person's view might have developed—so that you can learn about that person. This is a useful exercise because, if you have to try to reach an agreement with someone, it is important to understand what that person values (and the reasons they have formed their views). This will help you develop a solution that recognises not only your position and needs, but also the other person's position and needs. Listen to find out what is truly important to the other person (to determine whether you can address it in your solution).

Everyone has a bottom line. Listening carefully—rather than becoming rigid and unresponsive—will mean you can get to that bottom line much more easily. If you allow your own view to get in the way (usually fuelled by emotion), you can miss understanding the other person and his or her bottom line.

What is there to say sorry about? you ask.

I am going back to that argument that made you feel upset. There is real strength in understanding that part of the reason the argument happened in the first place was because you were trying to force the other person to view things your way. You didn't listen to his or her point of view and try to understand it (or even accept that the person is entitled to have his or her own views).

In apologising to that person, you are not saying you were wrong in your view. Rather, you are saying the following: *I am sorry for not listening and accepting that you are just as entitled to have a point of view as I am.*

Why is it so important to do this?

Think about it: when you get upset in a situation (such as an argument), you feel all sorts of physical symptoms that don't feel great, right?

Some people get anxious. Some get increased heart rates or blood pressure. Some get headaches, migraines, nausea, or a whole array of other physical effects. Who is the person that is being affected in this way? *You!*

The *only* person you are hurting is yourself—all because you were so entrenched in your point of view. Hardly worth it, right?

By recognising that we are not going to agree with everyone—and that there will always be other people who see things with different eyes and in different ways—and accepting that they are just as entitled as we are to a point of view, we will understand that there is no need to change anyone.

The real trick is to actually accept this truth and listen to the other person. Ask him or her what it is that led to a particular view and try to understand it.

Even if you don't agree with it, just accept it and agree to disagree about it. Sometimes you can only agree to disagree within yourself. There is no need to reach an agreement with the other person to agree to disagree. That other person might not be as enlightened as you—still stuck with his or her own negative barriers and misconceptions. There is no need for you to change the other person. The only person you need to worry about is you (in terms of changing yourself so you can let go of the negative and move on). No need to worry whether others are doing that too—that isn't your problem or issue. It is not your job to unblock others. Just focus on unblocking yourself so you can be clear to allow the positive to take over.

This is why apologising is so important. It is about you letting go of the issue that caused the conflict.

What might be surprising to you is that it doesn't only free *you* up, it can also have the very pleasant effect of allowing the other person to let go. It can clear the air around you both and allow you to move forward in your relationship with each other—whatever that relationship might be. Don't be afraid to be the first to apologise, even if you think your point of view was right. Remember that what you are saying sorry for is not allowing the other person to have his or her own view—and not validating the other person by listening.

People love to be listened to. Don't you?

By simply listening to others and accepting that they have their own perspectives, you can create feelings of goodness within others, and you can experience the positive effects of those feelings. Everyone wins!

You'll be surprised to learn that most people will repay the act of listening when they are done speaking. Be patient. It's like I said: not everyone will be on your level in terms of clearing the path to happiness. Just remind yourself mentally of this when you come across people who might seem difficult or stuck or stubborn. They have their own issues to resolve. It is not about you; it's about them and their own barriers, which they need to work on. They may never get to work on them. But again, remind yourself that this is not your problem to solve. Just focus on clearing your own path.

At first, it might not seem natural for you to think this way. But if you start to feel worked up about an issue, the first step is to breathe and take a mental time out.

If you snap and say something that attacks another person's point of view, be aware of your actions and apologise as soon as you recognise your mistake. Next, you need to tell the person that you accept how they feel and ask him or her to finish telling you his or her point of view. Listen!

If you wish, you can then tell that person that you have your own feelings and views. You can tell the person that you don't expect him or her to change views, but all you ask is for the other person to listen and accept that you have your *own* feelings and views. How much simpler your life will be when you practise doing this!

I know that whenever I come across people with views I don't hold myself, I just remind myself that they are entitled to have their own views. The natural urge to convince them of my views eventually dissipates. It just takes practise! And soon you will realise that all of those feelings that arise when you used to get upset—because someone would not change his or her views—just aren't there anymore. You don't have that need to change another's view anymore! And the sooner you say sorry to the person for not accepting that he or she is entitled to his or her own view, the better you will feel!

It's like I said, when you validate someone by saying, "Hey, I accept you have your own view" and, "I am happy to listen to you and validate that this is how *you* feel," you are more likely to receive a more positive response. There is no longer a need for either of you to become upset.

But what about people who try to change your views? Listen to what they have to say, and try to understand where they are coming from. Don't take it personally. Instead, sit back like an observer and assess it. Ask yourself, "Are there things that I can learn from this person and his or her point of view?"

Even if there aren't, at least you have assessed it and allowed that person to share his or her views with you. Always look for ways to learn new things and grow from the experiences of others.

Is Your Glass Full Yet?

At this point in this book, how far do you think you have come? When you look at the half-filled glass of water, do you think it's full, half-full, or half-empty?

If you are starting to see it as full, you are well on your way towards happiness. If you are seeing it as half-full, working towards seeing it as full will be an easier task for you. If you are thinking its half-empty, you still have a little work to do—but you will get there. It just takes time and practise.

When you see the glass as full, you have a good chance of seeing the world around you in a positive way. If you have looked at the glass and thought, *It is half-full of water,* you have found one of the positive characteristics that it has—it has water in it. You just have to remind yourself each time you see the glass that it is also full of air.

This process is about looking at what most would consider the negative aspect of a situation and seeing it as positive. Most "half-full people" would subconsciously think that the rest of the glass is half-empty without saying it. This is still a negative that sits in your subconscious mind and creates a barrier that holds you back—even if you don't realise at the time that this is what is happening. The trick is to consciously say to yourself, *I see the water, but I also see the air ... and both are positives in this glass.* The same holds true in life.

Learn to not only see the obvious positive characteristic of the situation, but also to say to yourself, "What else is there that is positive about this situation that might not be so obvious?" and "What might others consider negative about this situation?" After, you can look for the positive in that supposedly negative characteristic too.

Always keep in mind that *every* experience—even if others might consider it to be negative—has a positive characteristic. At the very least, it will teach you something about yourself, another person, or the situation itself.

This is not a skill that comes naturally to most people. Western culture has conditioned us to want more—we always look for what we don't have (and look for ways to get it). But the problem with this is that we forget to appreciate the things we do have in the process of striving for more. Life then passes us by, and we wonder why we're not happy. It's because you have forgotten to be happy with what you have and see that you have lots already! If not material things, you have life. Don't forget this. This is the most important thing you can possess in this world. This is the starting point.

People have become too obsessed with working and earning money to buy a better car, a bigger house, a bigger TV. They want more and more and more. People even go into incredible amounts of debt so they can have more.

Few people say, "I am so lucky. Look at what I have; I have enough." Not many people possess such a skill. Everyone is so busy looking for more and wanting more—do they stop and look at the positive things in their lives? More often than not, they don't.

The secret to being happy is actually being happy with what you have—no matter what that is. Like I said, my five-year-old daughter often says, "Get what you get and don't be upset."

You can still work hard and earn money, and you can still enjoy your money. But the secret to being truly happy is accepting whatever the universe sends your way—money, a child, a partner, the gift of health after a period of illness, etc. And once you accept these gifts, you must be grateful. Don't focus on getting more. Just allow it to come into your life and enjoy it for what it is at that time. Live life in the moment and enjoy what it has to offer as those moments move from one to the next.

If you learn to move from one moment to the next with gratitude and acceptance and see the positive each moment has to offer—whether it is a material possession or emotional or spiritual growth—you can't be anything but happy. You will be deriving joy and positivity from every moment. It would be impossible not to be happy when you're not constantly worrying about what you don't have and what the future does or does not hold for you. Just enjoy and learn from the moments as they present themselves to you. This is the way to grow.

One way of starting this process in your mind is to remind yourself to be grateful each day. You can start by saying, "Thank you for my life!" every morning when you awake.

Some people die in their sleep, so it is a wonderful thing to wake up alive each day. Say thank you for this gift of another day of life. Remember that life is a miracle in itself. It is something to be thankful for.

Another thing you can do is write yourself little reminders in your diary on your iPad, computer, or phone (or on little sticky tabs placed around your home or office that say, "Thank you for my life" or other positive things you want to be reminded of. I actually set up my Blackberry's diary to send me a reminder at 8 a.m. every day. It says, "Life is wonderful and full of abundance!" I have set the reminder to go off fifteen minutes before the entry every morning. It reminds me to be thankful. It opens the channels in my life (kind of like a radio picking up radio waves) allowing the positive energy of the world to flow towards me. It reminds me that every day my glass *is* full of things for me to be grateful for.

So, pull out your phone or open up your diary and make sure you receive those reminders! Remind yourself every day what you have to be thankful for. For example, your reminders could say the following:

"Thank you for the gift of life."

"My life is full of experiences and lessons that will help me grow."

"Thank you for my family. I'm so lucky to have them in my life."

"I am a beautiful person and appreciate who I am and the beauty I have within."

"I accept my life and everything it has to offer me."

"I accept into my life all the world has to offer me and am grateful for each moment and experience that is sent to me."

Another way of seeing the positive in every situation is to train yourself to speak in positive ways. When people ask you how you are doing, smile and say, "I'm great! What a great day!" I have heard so many people say, "Not bad!" or "I'm all right." But when you say things like that, you are not acknowledging or remembering that you actually have much to be grateful for.

When you say "I'm great" or something that acknowledges all of the positive around you (which in turn acknowledges that your glass is actually full), you will actually feel good. You will actually feel lifted and positive. The more you see the world in this positive way, the more positive you will feel.

Another good idea is to stop and think when someone asks you how your day was. Look for the positive things that happened that day. If you came across someone who appeared to be difficult to deal with, your answer might be "It was great. I learned how to deal with an interesting situation" or "I learned that I am very lucky not to have barriers in my life that can make me be negative to others. I am so lucky." Or you might say, "I came across Fred, and Fred was having a hard day. Even though he was allowing it to affect him and trying to pass that on to me, I learned that I can let that pass over me and move forward." Or you can just say, "I'm great" and silently acknowledge all the positive things you learned or derived from that day. This tactic is superior to launching into a speech about how bad your day was or how difficult Fred was. The only person you harm by responding in this negative way is you—doing so forces you to

Gigi G.

keep the negative within you. And while it stays within you, it will always make you feel negative—tired, unhappy, stressed, or any other negative feeling or symptom.

The secret is to stop and think before you talk, and make sure that each time you talk, you talk and think in a positive way. Words and thoughts are incredibly powerful. They multiply in effect, so it is really important to make sure they multiply in positive ways and not negative ways.

Here's one technique which really works. It is something I learned from the family of my 5-year-old's best friend at school. When you're sitting to have a meal, whether it's alone or with your family or friends, before eating, go around the table and ask each person *What was your favourite part of the day today?* One-by-one each person reflects on his or her day to draw the positive from it, so it can be put into positive words and shared with the others. Even if you are alone, you can use this technique. It is such a simple and effective way of focusing on the positive and being grateful for it.

Just try it and keep practising at it! You will soon realise how amazing and wonderful your life can feel and become when you view everything with such positivity and match that view with positive thoughts and words.

Look at the View from the Penthouse, Not the Basement!

What does this mean? Let me give you an example. Life and how we experience it completely depends on how *you* view it. I think I have made this point pretty clear.

How you view life (and what exists and happens around you) is your choice completely. Only you can truly control your mind. Others can't step into your mind and force you to see life in a certain way—unless you choose to allow them to do this, unless you choose to adopt what they are telling you. But ultimately, you have the power to choose whether or not to allow others to influence you and your perspective.

Metaphorically, you can choose to hop in the lift and take a ride to the penthouse of a 100-storey building and look at the amazing view from there. Alternately, you can take the lift to the basement many floors below ground where there is no light and there are no windows. Doing the latter will mean completely missing out on the amazing view more than 100 storeys above you.

This is your choice. It is always your choice. You have the buttons in front of you. Even if the lift is full of people and you can't reach the buttons easily, you can choose to say, "Excuse me" as you reach past them to press that button. Otherwise, you can ask someone to press it for you. But ultimately, your actions will dictate where you go. Even if the lift doesn't go all the way to the penthouse, you can still take the steps or find another way to get up there. Nothing is impossible. It all comes down to what *you* choose to do, and how *you* choose to get there.

It goes without saying that when you choose to view the world from the penthouse, the view is amazing. You can see so many marvels around you. You can see the big picture, and this can be an amazing and enlightening sight.

Even when there is a storm, from such an amazing vantage point the storm is beautiful. As you watch the storm, you may feel a little fear. But if you surrender that fear, you can watch the wonder of the storm itself, watch it pass, and see how it clears the air, allowing the sun to come out again and shine brilliantly. This is life!

Even when you are in the middle of what you might consider to be a storm, you can choose to detach yourself from it, stand above it (as if you were in a penthouse), watch it from above, look for and appreciate its purpose in your life, and watch the wonders unfold before you as the storm passes and the air clears. Knowing this is how the storm works—and that this is its purpose—makes being in a "life storm" so much easier to understand and withstand. You can always trust that the storm will pass, and surrendering any fear you might have about the storm—simply appreciating its beauty and purpose—will make any storm a positive experience for you.

But if you choose to sit in the eye of the storm and not step outside of it and appreciate its beauty and purpose, you miss the marvels it has to offer. The storm may tear you apart rather than uplift you. It is the very same storm that the person in the penthouse is seeing. But the experience for that person is more positive and loving because there is no fear and the view that person chose to take enabled that person to see the beauty and purpose of it. This is a choice. This is *your* choice.

Start taking that lift to the penthouse and seeing the view from the best room in the house. Start seeing the positive and wonder in everything you experience. Start seeing the big picture and how wonderful it is and can be. Your life will change in amazing ways.

Gigi G.

This world *is* an amazing place. It has so much good and positive to offer. If we all focus on the good—and enjoy and appreciate it (and allow others to enjoy and appreciate it)—what an amazing and positive world this place would be. This is your chance to start doing just that and encouraging others to do the same.

Before you know it, if we all do this, there will be no more war. There will only be good for us all to share. This is something amazing we can all work towards together. It starts with you and can multiply from you. You will see how amazing you will feel when you start thinking this way. You will start seeing how your thoughts can change your life and the lives of those around you. You will see how your thoughts can have a wave effect that travels from those near you to those near them and so on. What an amazing thing to be part of and to feel good about. You can do this and be part of this!

Just do it! Press that button and take your lift to the penthouse. Start enjoying the big picture. There is nothing to stop you but yourself.

If You Believe in Life, Life Will Believe in You!

Always remember the words in the title of this chapter. This idea is the most basic principle of your existence on this planet from which everything else in your life will stem.

What does it mean? It's as simple as this: we are all individuals in this life. At the end of the day, the one person in your life you know you can *always* count on is you. You are the person who is in control of your life.

You forge your own path in this life. You make the choices. Regardless of whether you like the outcomes of those choices, *you* made the choice. And the point of this life is to try to recognise the choices we made that had outcomes we liked. That way, we can repeat those choices to increase the outcomes we liked and recognise the choices that had outcomes we didn't like.

Gigi G.

Hopefully, in time, we learn to make (and recognise we *always* have the power to make) the most rewarding choices.

Ultimately, it doesn't matter whether anyone else on this planet believes in you and the choices you make. They don't control your life, *you* do.

It only matters that *you* believe in yourself and the choices you make in your life. Always remember this, because when you believe in yourself, life will believe in you and reward you with happiness, success, and self-fulfilment.

What does believing in yourself look like? It is being confident and knowing that you hold the key. It is choosing to be positive about your life and the experiences and situations that surround you. It is being confident enough to love and appreciate yourself (and the fact that you are unique and here for a reason). Everyone is here for a reason, and knowing that is a major step in accepting what life sends your way with gratitude. You can recognise that whatever is sent your way will help you achieve your life's purpose. It is about believing in yourself and accepting that everything in your life happens for a reason.

When you believe positive things are happening around and within you—and you believe your life is filled with positive experiences—your life will believe in you and multiply the positivity around and within you. The more you believe your life is positive, the more positive your life will be.

Freedom. What Is It?

I can tell you what freedom isn't. It isn't doing anything you like at any time, regardless of the other people around you. It isn't hurting others to benefit yourself.

Freedom is a state in which you have the ultimate ability to allow others to live their own lives, in which your actions cause no harm to others, and in which you are able to allow yourself to be free of negative energy and emotions (such as guilt, resentment, fear, hatred, anger, envy, jealousy, shame, and revenge).

Those negative feelings and reactions aren't much fun are they? But if you only saw the positive in everything and realised how much you had that was positive, you would have nothing to be guilty or resentful or angry about, would you? No, you wouldn't.

Understanding your feelings and emotions—knowing why you have them and allowing yourself to experience them without harming others (and while accepting others)—is freedom!

On your journey with me, you need to constantly practise at ridding yourself of negative energy.

Practise is the key!

But first, let's boost your self-worth. It is important to love yourself and feel worthy of freedom and happiness before you actually attain freedom and happiness.

First things first

Before working on your self-worth, be fully aware of your present reality and the forces of your past that have held you back. First, understand that these forces have held you back, stopping your life from moving forward. You can't give energy forward and backwards at the same time, can you? You go nowhere that way. This is the universe's very first and most fundamental law. Remember this if you ever feel like you are stuck.

You are probably in the middle of a tug of war between the feelings that are holding you back and your desire to move forward.

Let go of the feelings holding you back. Like a game of tug of war in which your opponent lets go of the rope, you will thrust forward to where you really want to be.

Sit down and write out the things you know and feel are emotionally holding you back and creating feelings within you that are unpleasant. Write down the feelings about yourself and others that are problematic. List all the issues that you have found hard to resolve within yourself in a positive way. List the things that you haven't been able to resolve with others, things that make you feel depressed, and things that make you feel tired or stressed or any other negative emotion. Writing it all down allows you to get it all out. And then you can address each issue. Once you have this list, you are ready to move forward to the next step.

You can choose to feel worthy—it is *your* choice

Always remember that feeling worthy happens when you choose to feel that way. It is a state of mind that you can develop. All you need to do is feed yourself with positive messages and surround yourself with positive thoughts. To do this, you need to face your true feelings head-on and learn how to view them differently and positively. This is why you have the list—you can face each feeling head-on and challenge each feeling with a positive way of looking at it.

Gigi G.

What you need to know is that people sometimes view situations incorrectly—not as they really (objectively) are. Humans feel more comfortable believing their interpretations of their circumstances are correct. Their views are their security blankets. They let them escape from reality when they have not developed the tools to cope with reality. This is a distortion of perception.

For example, at the extreme, there are people with body dysmorphic disorder. At its very basic level, people with this disorder see themselves as hideous or deformed. But other people do not see them this way.

Another extreme example is a girl who suffers from anorexia. She views herself as fat when she looks at herself in the mirror. But in reality, she is grossly emaciated. Her existence is reduced to skin and bones. This is a reflection of not only her physical being, but also her emotional being.

She has reduced the amount of space she occupies in this world because she does not feel worthy of a grand and imposing existence. In effect, it is almost as though she does not want to be seen (by making herself so small)—facing reality would be too difficult. There is some reality that she is escaping from by using such distortions of her physical self.

When our views are not a reflection of our reality (when viewed objectively), it is a sign that there is a root issue we must explore.

In my experience, it usually comes down to not feeling worthy to experience life without distortion … free of the negative energy that leads to the distortion.

All the girl with anorexia needs to do is focus on the reasons why she doesn't feel worthy of occupying much space in this life. She needs to try to understand why she engages in this minimising behaviour. For every distorted message that she sends herself, there is a problem brewing under the surface that she chooses to ignore. The longer she ignores it, the more buried it becomes. This means it gets harder and harder to dig the issues up and face them. It becomes much easier for her to minimise herself because there is less effort involved—no digging to do. Believe me—that girl used to be me, many lifetimes ago.

I used to lack self-love, and I didn't know how to see through the negative cloud that I chose to live in for many years. This was very strange because I had such a loving, supportive, and caring family. I had (and still have) incredibly caring, kind, and generous parents who are amazing mentors in my life. I have a wonderful sister who loves me and is very kind.

So what led me down this path of negativity? When I was about eight years old, my ballet teacher (God rest her soul) made a comment about me to some other children. She said, "Who is this fat child?" This person was an adult, so I paid attention to the words that were said. I was only eight—I didn't understand that this adult may have had her own problems. I didn't know I could just choose to say, "That's what she says. Just because she says that, it doesn't make it true."

As I grew older, I came to know it wasn't my problem; it was her problem. I wasn't overweight. All I had to do was look at pictures of myself as a child. But for many years that followed, I allowed that comment to affect me. I felt so ashamed of myself that I didn't want to eat. I didn't want my friends to see me changing in the change rooms when we went swimming or got ready for physical education at school. I now understand that what I was doing was trying to make myself smaller and less noticeable to others so people didn't feel the need to attack or judge me.

After many years of being way too thin, I got tired and moody and depressed. It was a vicious cycle. I allowed that one comment to eat me away physically, emotionally, and mentally. I had given so much power to those few words and allowed them to take over my existence.

If I had made the choice to push those words aside and say, "It really doesn't matter what you think or say. I love myself, and that is all that matters" my life for those early years would have been very different. My head would not have been in the negative clouds, blocking my ability to view the positive in the world and myself.

Some people might say, "How awful. Do you wish that you knew the secret to seeing your glass as full back then?" My answer to that question is, "No, I do not."

That whole experience, I have since come to recognise, was a positive one. It taught me all I know now. It taught me that when you allow yourself to see the negative, the negative takes over your existence and breeds. It taught me that viewing the world with negative eyes—seeing and focusing on the negative—has an effect on your psyche and body. That perspective can prevent you from feeling good and being happy. I learned that it doesn't matter why people act the way they do. It is a waste of your energy to figure any of that out. It is better to accept that people behave in certain ways, which you cannot control. The person you can control is yourself. You can choose how you view, and react to, each situation—and how you deal with others.

The experience I went through taught me that my instructor probably had issues of her own (which is true of many people). She might not have known how to be kind—perhaps because she was never taught how to be kind or because she had never been treated kindly.

To this day, I don't know why she said that to me—but now I know it doesn't matter. When you come across people you might consider to be difficult, just remind yourself that a person's behaviour comes from how he or she feels inside and his or her own issues. We are not all without issues. We all have a choice to deal with people with kindness or meanness.

We must understand that sometimes people behave poorly or negatively because there is something poor or negative within themselves (and there are issues that the person has to deal with). The sooner you understand this, the better. It is then much easier to not take on another person's behaviour. You might learn that a person is not happy. You might learn that you do not wish to be in a person's company anymore. You might learn that each time you come across a person, you know what to expect and understand it is not about you—this will make it easier not to take on any negative energy. You might learn that a person has issues that you can encourage them to talk about (that way, he or she can let go of the negative emotions and move forward). You might learn that certain behaviour makes others feel sad or negative. And you might learn that there are others who are not as equipped as you to learn from their experiences and move on. There are so many lessons you can learn from another's behaviour. Each lesson that presents itself to you is a positive because you grow from each lesson.

You see, people generally use forms of self-destructive behaviour and gross distortions of reality to allow themselves to escape and live a life that suits them. That life might not be about opening their eyes to see the beauty. Instead, it might be about closing their eyes and trying to escape the world. But the problems and issues never go away unless you face them and deal with them. They lurk below (or wherever else we have hidden or buried them), and they hold us down like an anchor, preventing us from being free of negative energy.

The true art of living is not to merely exist in this world, but to be brave and face those very problems or issues that hinder your life. The key is to stop yourself from pretending that problems don't exist. Begin living a life that is honest and true and free of the ghosts from the past that haunt you.

Letting go is the key!

There are many ways to let go. First, you need to sit down and write out those issues in your life that you feel affect you in a negative way. Are there people you feel have wronged you? Write those names down and write out what they said or did that affected you in a negative way. Ask yourself, *Am I truly free of this issue, or is it still with me?* If you have written it down, it is probably still an issue you carry with you.

Search for the truth in your early years and connect with reality. Try to ask yourself truthfully, *What perceptions of mine do I suspect (or know) might be distorted or not accurate?* Write them down and challenge them. Ask yourself why you have them. Look deep inside yourself and be honest with yourself. Try to see things as an observer of your life (from above yourself) and assess your thoughts and perceptions as an observer of them, no matter how painful it might be to do so. If you feel any pain, remember that pain exists only because you view the situation as negative. What you will work on after facing the truth is changing your perception of it, finding the positive in it. That way, you don't hurt anymore. But to be able to change your perception of those situations, you must face those situations. Otherwise, you won't be able to examine them and find out what is positive about them.

The key is to forgive yourself and others for your past experiences. This gives you the chance to let go of the negative energy and emotions that attach to them and hold you back from feeling worthy of a happy life filled with self-love.

What you are forgiving yourself for is not making the choice to be happy in the past and allowing the actions of others to dictate your life. Say it to yourself, "I forgive myself for making the choice to hold onto the past and view that past as negative" and, "I forgive myself for making the choice to view the actions or words of others as negative (and allowing those negative views to hold me back from being happy)."

Then you need to forgive those other people for their actions and words. You must recognise that they were just experiences in your life that you can learn from and which have shaped you as a person.

After this process of forgiveness, which is all about letting go of the negative attached to whatever or whomever you are forgiving, you can move on to the next step. You can learn something positive from those past experiences and give those experiences a positive spin in your life.

Those experiences will always be part of you (a part of what has shaped you to be the person you are right now), so the key is to replace the negative emotions attached to them with positive emotions.

The most basic positive emotion you can attach to those experiences is as follows: "Thank you for that experience. It has taught me about myself and about what I do or do not want from my life."

Once you are grateful for the experience, it is already turning into a positive one. And then the effect on you (at the level of how you feel about yourself) can change into a more positive one.

To grow in self-worth, you have to let go of the ease of living in and holding on to the past. It might be easier to just hold on to the past—it takes effort to let go of it. But the pay-off for that effort can be great!

The past, after all, is just history.

Accept, learn from, and let go of it.

The present and future are in your control.

Now Let's Move to the Next Step:
Your Feelings about Yourself!

Now you need to start loving yourself and accepting that you do deserve happiness.

Let's start with an exercise. Remember that exercise is the key!

Do this every day, every chance you get. Seize every opportunity that presents itself to you to practise.

Carpe diem!

(Seize the day!)

Go to your mirror and look at yourself as if you were looking at another person entirely. Forget it is actually you.

Now look at your features, your contours, the colour of your hair, your eyes, skin, etc. Get to know yourself as though you were getting to know someone new.

Now look at yourself in the eyes. Remember, when you look at people in the eyes, you connect with them. Look into your eyes as though you were looking into the eyes of someone else. They are the windows to a person's soul, so connect with those eyes.

Look into the eyes of that person in the mirror (and into that person's soul).

Now say, "I love you" to yourself while looking into your eyes. Now say, "You are such a beautiful person. I am so happy to know you." These are called positive affirmations. Why? Because you are sending positive messages to yourself that affirm the beauty and goodness that makes you who you are.

At first, you might feel silly doing this. I know I felt a little silly at first. But understanding why you feel silly is actually important. It means you're not comfortable with yourself, and you don't appreciate all the wonderful things that make you who you are.

Anything that embarrasses you in life and makes you feel silly is usually touching on a sensitive spot inside of you—and that is a sign that it is something you need to face with honesty. Ask yourself why it is that you feel those feelings, and then challenge them.

Gigi G.

Not being able to say that you love yourself is usually a sign that you do not feel worthy of happiness or self-love. But say to yourself that there really is no reason why you don't deserve to be happy and love yourself. You make up those reasons—usually based on negative emotions or views that you have about yourself (or situations that have shaped your perceptions). If you change those negatives into positives by challenging each negative and giving it a positive description, you really don't have any reason to feel unworthy, do you?

Keep practising. Say you love and appreciate yourself and say you deserve happiness. Redefine your experiences from negative ones into positive ones. By practising and continuing this process of positive affirmation and definition, you will connect with yourself. The positive affirmations will become part of your subconscious. Before you know it, you will start feeling very positive about yourself because you recognise the good in you.

Once you get to that point of loving yourself, you will start to see good and positive in everything—not only within you, but also in others and the things around you. It's because you're training your mind to seek beauty and search for the positive things or characteristics not only in yourself, but also in people, things, and situations.

Eventually, you will become comfortable with saying, "I love you" to yourself (even if silently, in your mind). You will realise that you will have much more self-love and self-appreciation, which will affect the way you see your life. Your life will be far more enjoyable and fulfilling than before because you will actually feel worthy of it.

Just another step on your journey to being free to be happy!

You'll learn to be free of the chains of negativity—and you can take another step towards your positive and happy life!

Let Go!

It's like I said before—and I keep coming back to it because it really is an important tool in reaching your happy life—you must let go of what's happened in the past. You must let go of the negative attached to the past.

As each second ticks by, it becomes your past. The key to living life and being happy is to live life in the moment and allow the past to become the past and stay there. This means also leaving any negative emotions attached to the past in the past. Why let them infect your enjoyment of the present? There's no sense in that.

In fact, the ultimate goal of life is to enjoy each moment, see the positive in each moment as it happens, allow the moments to pass, and try to make each moment better than the last. This is a wonderful skill and one of the greatest secrets to being happy.

The past is unchangeable. You have to accept that you just can't change it. Once the second has passed, you can't get it back. So, why waste your energy trying to change it (or wondering what it is you could have done to change it)? You just can't.

Make the decision to stop wasting your energy in this way. Make it now. Say to yourself,

> **"I accept the past and move forward**
> **knowing the past has brought me here.**
> **All is as it is meant to be."**

What you can control is the now and how you move forward in a positive way from the now (from one positive moment to the next). You also control how you learn and grow from each moment and what you take with you from each moment to the next.

You can also choose to welcome each moment with open arms and a smile. That is *your* choice. You can choose how you live that moment and how you view it. That, again, is *your* choice. The art of life is to teach yourself how to choose the most positive way to live and how to view each moment. When you choose to live each moment with a positive mind, acceptance, and a smile, the effect can only be a positive one. And that positive effect will radiate from you to those around you. It's quite infectious!

Gigi G.

So make the choice now! Take charge of your actions and your mind, and use them to direct your life forward and towards the positive.

Healing Wounds

Healing wounds is all part of the process of letting go. What do I mean by *wounds?*

Past experiences can be like deep cuts. Some cut deep into you and take a long time to heal (depending upon how you treat and care for them). Some people use stitches as an aid to the healing process, keeping the wound closed so it can heal properly. But leaving a wound untreated or pulling your stitches out really hinders the healing process—it will never heal if you keep reopening the wound. It can end up leaving some major scars if you keep pulling it open and don't treat it properly.

Life is exactly the same! Why pull out the stitches from your old wounds only to cause more pain and hurt?

So how do you treat the wounds from the past? The simple answer is to let go of them. But part of that process of letting go might need a little treatment and healing time to allow you to let go of it.

The Glass IS Full

One of the secrets to the letting go process is to always remember that an emotional or spiritual wound is a thing that can completely heal. Being kind to yourself is one of the treatments that will help your wound heal well.

This is why it is so important to face the unresolved issues from your past and treat and resolve them. Only then can you let them go with love and peace. Otherwise, they will keep coming back consciously or subconsciously in your life, affecting your relationships with others and preventing you from living and enjoying each moment.

It's like being in a room full of smoke. It's not a very good environment to have a relationship with someone, is it? They can't see you—the person you are—and your eyes are so full of smoke that you can't see yourself or others or your surroundings. You can actually lose yourself in the smoke. So how do you get rid of the smoke in the room? You've got to open the windows and doors and let some air in to clear the smoke. Only then can you see yourself and others and the wonderful and positive things around you in that room. That's exactly how life is.

If you don't face the wounds of the past (including the treatment and healing of them), learn from them, surround them with love and peace, and allow them to remain in the past with that love and peace attached to them—if you don't do all that, the room that is your life will be clouded like a room full of smoke. If you look for the positive things you learned from that experience and accept it with love, you can open the windows and allow the air to take it out of your room. That will allow your room to clear! It's that simple! When your life is truly clear of those experiences, and you move forward in your life with the positive things you gained from those experiences, there is no reason your life would not be positive!

Past experiences—painful or good—will always teach you valuable lessons about yourself and your life. From them, you can learn ways to improve and love yourself.

Part of that process is forgiving those people you feel have let you down or hurt you in the past. (The process can also include forgiving yourself for things you have not been able to live with until now.) This is the process of opening up the windows and doors and letting the air clear. As the air clears, you are no longer choked by the smoke. You are giving yourself the chance to breathe clearly.

The same goes for the process of forgiveness. By forgiving others and yourself, you are letting go of all those negative emotions and energies that felt like wounds in your life. You are letting go of emotions which have clouded your life all this time.

What other negative emotions do you need to let go of to allow those wounds to heal and truly be a thing of the past?

Fear is one such emotion.

We sometimes find ourselves going through life with fears about what will happen to us—the elusive "what if?"

The more you fear something, the more likely your fears will come true. When you are so focused on something, you are likely to make it happen.

Fear is a negative energy that we throw out from ourselves, and it boomerangs right back at us until we let go of it. But how do you get over the fear? Again, letting go and not focusing on what you fear is a great start. When you let go of something, it is no longer attached to you.

There are many ways of getting over fears. Here are some examples that seem to work. Use what works best for you.

One technique is to face the fear. For instance, a person who is afraid of heights will first step up onto a small stepladder until he or she is comfortable with that height. Once comfortable, the next step can be taken. Each step might be a small one, but eventually the steps are going to get that person onto the balcony of a second-storey apartment. A bit higher and the nerves are on edge, but looking down, facing the fear, and realising there actually is nothing to fear each time a step is taken is a great way to just challenge the fear and allow it to disappear.

Gigi G.

When the fear disappears, the person is going to feel great; exhilarated, and probably full of adrenalin and endorphins. Why? Because the fear is gone! The negative energy that the person has held onto is gone!

Each step you take to challenge your fears in life might have your adrenalin pumping and your heart pounding, but there is no greater feeling than the feeling of letting go of this fear. Nothing feels better than conquering a fear and not letting it hold you back any longer.

The person who has a fear of heights finally gets to the plane and is strapped to the back of a skydiving instructor. The fear is gone now. And when the person falls out of the plane, the person is free of fear and able to look down on the world below and enjoy the pure beauty of it. And the person can enjoy the ride too! This is the secret to life—letting go of the fears that cloud your life and vision and learning how to enjoy the view and the ride. It is that simple: whatever you fear, face it!

Feel it and recognise that it is a normal reaction. With this understanding, you allow the fear to take its course and leave you. If you hold on to the fear, it will never leave you—you will never be able to enjoy your life. It will stop you from enjoying the view and the ride of life.

The same goes for challenging and letting go of other negative thoughts and feelings you might experience on your journey through life. Always remember that they are just your thoughts and feelings based on the way you have viewed your life to date.

Once you change how you view life—once you learn that life is a bunch of moments that present lessons and opportunities—you will no longer have the negative thoughts and feelings. You will have no negative perceptions to create them.

So when you have negative thoughts—for example, "I'm so fat" or "I'm so stupid" or "Nothing ever works out for me" or "My life is a nightmare"—say to yourself straight away, "What am I saying?" Challenge yourself. Remind yourself that you can choose to see your life in a different way ... a more positive way.

Look for a positive thing to be happy about and remind yourself of those positive things you have to be thankful for. For instance, "I have nice eyes" or "I have a great smile" or "I have two arms and two legs and my body is intact. I am so lucky to be able bodied and living in a country where I am free to be me." There is *always* something to be grateful for! The simple fact that you are alive, wake up each morning, and continue breathing is the most basic thing to be thankful for.

Gigi G.

Any positive thought will override a negative one. Say and think positive things to yourself all the time—they will lead you to positive experiences in your life. Think positive, and you and your life will be positive.

Remember that challenging, healing, and letting go of the fears and the negative thoughts and feelings that have held you back in your life (and doing this with love, acceptance, care, and kindness to yourself) will clear out the smoke that is clouding up your life. Going through this process will allow you to see the great things within and around you. Life can be nothing but positive with such a great and clear place to experience it from.

"The Tree"

Are you baffled by the title of this chapter? I bet you are. What do I mean by *The Tree*?

It's a wonderful little thing I say to myself when I want or need to remind myself of how wonderful the world is and how lucky I am to be a part of it. Yes, *The Tree*.

There is a tree outside my favourite local cafe. When I have a chance to go to my cafe, I love to sit outside and look at this tree. Why? Ever heard the phrase, "The best things in life are free"? It is *so* true!

People spend millions and millions of dollars on art—paying for a picture of a real life object or moment, such as a tree or a parade. But people forget that the real work of art is around them every day, and it costs them nothing to enjoy or appreciate. The pure art of nature and the world is all around us.

Gigi G.

When I look at this tree, I feel so inspired by the beauty of it. The way the light shines on the leaves, the brilliant shades of green of the leaves, the rustle of the wind through the leaves—it is so beautiful to watch and listen to. And so many people walk past this tree as they type on their phones and block out the beautiful sounds it makes with their earphones. They don't appreciate its beauty. They are missing out!

The other thing about this tree is that I marvel at the way the light shines on its leaves and feeds it, allowing it to grow. When nature is nurtured, it thrives! We are part of nature, so when we nurture ourselves with the wonderful things the breath of life (not things) has to offer, we can grow and thrive too.

The beauty of the world is all around you, and it costs nothing. Every time I look around me—whether it's out my window at the world outside or at the sky or at the trees along the path walking to work—I see a work of art. It is absolutely amazing how taking the time to see and appreciate the beauty around you can make you feel so good!

I was speaking to a friend one morning. Coincidentally, it happened to be at my café. I said, "The secret to being happy is so very simple. Each day I take the time—no matter where I am—to say thank you for the beauty of the world around me. It's amazing how taking the time to actually see the world as a work of art can really make you feel so good. And it's all for free! How lucky we are to have such beauty around us at our fingertips. All we have to do is remind ourselves to look at it, and appreciate it." The effect of saying "thank you" is profound! I know it has an effect on me every time I say it because it's so true. But there were tears in his eyes, and he thanked me for making him feel so good. It was that easy to—as he said—make his day. And it is that easy to make your own day, each and every minute. The words and concepts are so simple, yet so powerful! It really is that easy.

Also remember that our bodies are equipped to make us feel good. Our own endorphins and opiates and adrenalin can work wonders. I have never tested it scientifically, but I always feel like I have a rush of endorphins and natural opiates in my body when I take the time to enjoy the tree.

So, when I say, *The Tree* to myself, it is a reminder to enjoy life and the beauty of nature and everything else around me. I don't just mean the tree outside my cafe, I mean everything in nature that surrounds all of us. It is all free. And when you take the time to look at it and enjoy the beauty of it, you can feel nothing but good.

I honestly think that people who take illegal drugs to numb themselves are truly missing out. If they looked at the tree, they could see it for the beautiful thing that it is and allow their own bodies to take over and make them happy. Those people numb their feelings and prevent themselves from feeling, viewing, and enjoying life.

If you are struggling with illegal drugs or alcohol, remember that they are stopping you from seeing *The Tree*. They are stopping you from enjoying the real world and preventing your own body's chemicals from releasing and making you feel good. They are numbing you and taking away your ability to *truly* feel good within (and about) yourself. They are stopping you from experiencing life in a clear room. They might feel good at the time (because they take you away and help you escape whatever fear or pain you are hiding from), but all they do is mask and smoke up your life.

The only way to clear the air in your room is to get rid of the substances and remind yourself that they stand in the way of you living your life and seeing life as the wonderful vault of experiences that it is. Sign up for that rehab program and get started. Clear everything out and start enjoying your tree!

Time out!

Every now and again, it is really important to take some time out to regroup, think, or simply give yourself to the moment.

Sometimes life can race past when we are busy. Haven't you noticed how quickly life speeds by when you are busy? Before you know it, you're tired and haven't enjoyed yourself.

The art of life is to take time out to enjoy it. The trick is to live your life like this—make time to take a moment and enjoy life.

How do I do it? I try to listen to a song that I really enjoy and sing along. I sing in the shower a lot! I might turn my stereo system on, put on my favourite music, and allow myself to really feel the music—even if just for a few minutes.

Gigi G.

At lunch, when I'm not in court, I might just sit in the park across from the courthouse and soak up some sun. I might go for a walk and remind myself of how blessed I am to be alive. I might look at a picture of my husband and my kids and remind myself of how lucky I am to have them.

If I'm outside, I will look at the sky and see how magnificent it is—appreciating nature like a work of art. I observe the colours and shades, listen to the wind blowing, and look at the way the light shines on the leaves of the trees as the wind moves through them. If I am at home, I will pull a chair outside, sit in it, close my eyes, and listen to the sounds of the birds—or just meditate. Better still, I might cuddle with my children or husband—whatever presents itself to me in the moment.

The secret of life is to seize and enjoy the moments that present themselves to you (and make sure that you give yourself the time to enjoy those moments). Even if you start with taking just a few minutes out of each day to regroup, smile, and remind yourself to look for the positive angle in what you are doing at the time, that's enough. As you become more practised at finding a few moments each day to do this, you will find that you will do it more and more each day. Eventually, the concept of taking time out to draw the best of each moment that you live will become part of who you are and how you live life each day.

At first, it might seem like an effort to take time out and appreciate the moment for what it is. It might seem taxing to appreciate who you are, but remember there is plenty of time. It doesn't take long to find time to appreciate yourself and the fact that you have life. This is something you can do every moment of the day.

It's just a matter of practise!

Take Steps Forward
with Courage

Many years ago now, I got a tattoo of the Japanese character for courage on the top of my right foot—my dominant foot, the one I take my first step forward with.

Why did I do this? To remind myself that the only way forward is to take a step in that direction—forward—with courage. Whether physically or metaphorically, the only way forward is to keep moving generally in that direction with courage, strength, passion, and conviction. Be confident in each step you take.

The steps don't have to be the size of leaps in order to be successful steps forward in your life. Baby steps are just as effective and valuable. In fact, it's usually the baby steps that we take when the steps feel harder to take. This is when you need and use your courage the most. If you remember that courage is the key to taking each of those steps—and trust that when you have that courage you can move forward towards your ultimate goal of happiness—you can move towards that goal in a happy and positive way. You can move forward with conviction that each step is what gets you there. You just need to find ways to remind yourself to be brave.

So what is it you need the courage for?

You sometimes need courage to help you step out of a place of self-doubt or fear of the unknown. You sometimes need it to let go of those barriers or emotions or feelings that hold you back—those obstacles that stop you from moving forward in your life.

Part of the secret to this process of letting go and moving forward in a positive way is to sit down and figure out what those barriers (or negative emotions or feelings) are. Once you know what they are, you can start taking steps to move away from them, let go of them, and move past them.

It's like I said before, a clear path is much easier to navigate. The whole point is to avoid (or navigate around) the obstacles. The more you clear those obstacles away, the easier the path will become.

Gigi G.

The task is to figure out what is blocking your path on your life journey. Only then can you face the obstacles with courage, move them out of the way, and move along your path more easily.

Being free of those barriers will allow you to freely enjoy the journey for what it is (and the wonderful lessons and experiences it has to offer).

As you do this, always remember that the lessons in life (and the experiences of our life) are received by moving those barriers and moving past them. You learn a lot about yourself and who you are when you face your obstacles. You must understand and accept that facing those obstacles is part of your journey. Each time you face and move them, the experience of doing so will have a positive effect on you—you will learn something from them. Once you understand and accept this, it is easier to move or get around those barriers. It is easier because you embrace the challenge and know that all you have to do is face it, accept that it is there, and move it out of the way (or step around or over it).

The basic principle to remember is that there is a solution to everything in life when you live with courage, love, and acceptance. Courage is evident when you live life with love and acceptance. You will navigate the path with greater peace, giving you joy and happiness that money just can't buy.

You need to find ways to remind yourself each day that you need to have courage in every step you take in life. This is why I got my tattoo.

But you don't have to go out and get a tattoo! Do what works for you. There are so many other ways to remind yourself to be courageous and brave while navigating the road that is your life.

When I was younger—before my tattoo—the way I reminded myself of this was to place little sticky tabs wherever I went. The sticky tabs said, "Move forward with love and courage." I would write the message in my diary and place the tabs on different objects at work and at home. Actually, I still do this. I have the sticky tabs in my wallet and around my computer screen, and I even have recurring messages in my phone's calendar that remind me to be brave. The messages say,

"Live your life with courage!"

"A life lived is a life full of courageous moments."

People ask me all the time what my tattoo on my foot means. They also ask about all my sticky tabs. When I tell them, I always get an amazing reaction. It is almost like they are realising that life can be that simple.

Gigi G.

It's very satisfying to be able to share this philosophy with them and with you because it really is that simple. Being happy can be that simple. You just have to remind yourself that it is all about moving forward and being brave enough to let go of the negative feelings and thoughts you have every now and again. It is all about knowing that the negative will hold you back—and letting go of the negative will allow you to move forward ... free of that negative energy. It makes complete sense that, when you move forward without the negative chained to you, your life is going to feel a lot lighter and more free. You will feel free to be happy and experience life.

"Things Don't Matter, People Matter"

Respect for people is something I taught my girls when they were very young—young enough to understand the concept. It is incredible when I hear them say it to each other all the time now. And they are only five and seven!

And how true it is! It is such an important thing to remind yourself of each and every day.

What life (and your happiness) really comes down to is a recognition of the fact you are alive, healthy, and able to be yourself. Those are the most important things in life. And if you have family, their health and security are also more important than anything you could possibly own in your life. Things don't make you who you are. What you have in life (in terms of objects and property), doesn't make you who you are.

Gigi G.

In fact, it doesn't matter what you have in life if you're not a kind, honest, and genuine person. And you must be kind, honest, and genuine not only to others, but also to yourself.

You need to accept that people who are only interested in knowing you if you have status, wealth, fame, or fortune are simply not your true friends. The people who are true friends are the ones who want to know you regardless of what you have and who you are in terms of position or fame.

An essential part of leading a happy life is to surround yourself with those friends who love you for who you are as a person, not what you have. Another major key to leading a happy life is to accept yourself for who you are as a person—and to avoid making any apologies to anyone for what you do or do not have in terms of material things. Never apologise for not having a big house or a luxury car. Feeling the need to apologise for what you do or do not have is just another type of negative energy that holds you back from being happy.

People become obsessed with having things, thinking it will make them happier … but it doesn't. If you don't have the money for something, does that make you a bad person? No! That's ridiculous. If you can't have a house on the water with a boat and a Ferrari, does that mean you have no value as a person? Absolutely not!

Your worth in this life—to yourself and to others—comes from within you. Your value as a human being comes from who you are as a person—your character, your integrity, your actions, and the words you choose to describe yourself and others.

I always say to my girls (especially when they are having a typical children's grumble about not having the latest game or toy), "It doesn't matter what you have or what you look like if you're not ..." and then I pause and wait for them to finish the sentence. You know what they always finish my sentence with? The word *kind*. It is so true. It doesn't matter what you have or what you look like, if you're not kind. You must be kind to yourself and kind to others.

Being kind to yourself and others—and being thankful for those things that matter, such as the fact that you're alive—is the most important thing in life. If all of us took this message to heart and lived life with that philosophy, what an amazing place the world would be.

This doesn't mean you can't have all the latest and most expensive gadgets and houses and cars and things, it just means that you need to understand that it's not important to have them. It doesn't make you who you are inside. There are many people with everything (in the material sense) who are so unhappy—and some who are not so nice or kind. The stuff doesn't change this. The stuff is just *stuff*.

Gigi G.

Your journey in this life is about being the most positive, kind and thankful person you can be, viewing life as an opportunity and experience, and being truly grateful for every little thing you have. It is also about knowing that you don't need stuff to be happy (and learning to completely rely on yourself and the person within you for your happiness).

So, if you find yourself feeling unhappy or negative because you don't have something, stop yourself and say, "Things don't matter, people matter." You have the breath of life at the very least, and that is such a huge thing to be thankful for. Material things just can't buy you that. Always remind yourself of this fact.

Risky Business

Risk is a part of life.

Without taking risks, you can never be free!

So what do I mean by risk?

I don't mean dangerous risks such as walking in front of a train or a bus. I am talking about being yourself (and being true to yourself)—taking the risk to live!

There is a poem my mother made me read when I was younger. It was written by an anonymous author. At one stage, my mother made me print it out for her so she could place it on her fridge. It is still there!

Gigi G.

It is a wonderful piece that really says a lot about the freedom gained by taking risks in life. The message is so simple: risk is a natural and freeing part of life.

Read this poem every time you are having trouble moving forward or making decisions in your life—it will inspire you to take the chance to be yourself and live your life.

> To laugh is to risk appearing a fool.
>
> To weep is to risk appearing sentimental.
>
> To reach out for another is to risk involvement.
>
> To expose feelings is to risk exposing your true self.
>
> To place your ideas, your dreams before a crowd
> is to risk their loss.
>
> To love is to risk not being loved in return.
>
> To live is to risk dying.
>
> To hope is to risk despair.
>
> To try is to risk failure.
>
> But risks must be taken, because the greatest hazard in life is to risk nothing.
>
> The person who risks nothing, does nothing, has nothing, and is nothing.

> We may avoid suffering and sorrow, but we simply cannot learn, feel, change, grow, love, or live.
>
> Chained by our certitudes, we are a slave;
> we have forfeited our freedom.
>
> Only a person who risks is truly free.

The message is so clear, isn't it? If you don't take the risk to feel love, if you don't try, if you don't take the risk to live your life, you have already failed. You haven't even given yourself the chance to succeed. The success is in the trying, not the outcome.

Each time you try, you learn what the outcome will be. And then you can decide if that is the outcome you truly want to pursue. If not, you can try at other things until you get the outcome you desire. By trying, you always gain something. At the very least, you gain the knowledge of what that particular path can hold for you. Without that knowledge, you are left for the remainder of your life wondering what could have been if you had only tried.

By trying, you answer that question. You can move on to the next chapter of your life. And each time you move onto the next chapter— and keep taking those risks—you can reach the outcome you desire. And whether it happens straight away or takes some time, the most important thing is the journey. It is only through trying and taking those risks to be your true self, to seek the happy life you desire, that you can give yourself the chance to succeed.

Gigi G.

So, step forward into that next chapter of your life with the courage to take those risks in life. Enjoy the journey that follows for what it is: your journey. Because only those who take those risks to be truly happy—to break the chains of the past that hold them back—can truly be free. Have courage knowing that you deserve happiness. There is no reason why you don't deserve happiness. Everyone does! You just have to believe it and enjoy the ride on the way there!

Every Childhood Has Its Ups and Downs

At this point in your journey with me, some of you might say, "But so many bad things have happened to me. How can I let go of all those things?"

First of all, you are not alone. You can rest assured that no matter what has happened to you, it is in the past. You can choose to leave it there and move on.

What you can also feel comforted by is the fact that very few people have no emotional challenges in their lives. Everyone in this world has skeletons in the closet. You are not alone. One thing that can hold you back is feeling like you are the only one who has felt a certain way. Everyone goes through moments of feeling trapped, held back, or clouded by the blackness of the energy that can come from negative emotions. I have!

Gigi G.

It is the way you deal with those moments that makes all the difference. It is also how you equip yourself to deal with those moments that makes all the difference.

If you remind yourself that you are truly worthy of being happy, you can use your experiences to positively develop your personality and life.

Those people who don't believe they are worthy of happiness are simply chaining themselves to those negative feelings coming from emotional experiences. They are allowing themselves to be held back by them. Does that make sense?

It's like I said: you need to first believe and understand that you deserve happiness. Everyone does. And no matter what might have happened to you in the past—no matter what traumas you may have experienced in your past—they are all lessons in life. Those experiences shaped the person you are today; they all can teach you what you do and do not want in your life. Those experiences can also teach you how you should treat others in life. There is always a positive message that comes from past experiences. That is an important key to being happy. Remember that how you learn and grow from those experiences is always *your* choice. Living your life with that knowledge is true freedom.

Live Life in the Moment! Make the Most of the Now!

Make things happen for yourself. Things won't just happen for you, so there is no point grumbling about things not going your way.

You have to put your positive energy into the world so it can take it and throw it back your way. This is such a basic law of nature. What you throw into it will come back at you like a boomerang. Make sure you throw your positive energy out there, because this law of nature applies to both types of energy, positive and negative.

If you throw your negative energy and feelings out into the world, they will come back at you and hit you twice as hard (because you are already down when it comes back to you and hits you).

But when you throw your positive energy and feelings out there, they will come back at you. And because you are already positive, they will make you feel even more positive. And that positivity will keep multiplying.

That's why people who constantly throw negative energy into the universe seem to spiral into the depths of despair and oblivion, getting more and more negative. Every time they throw negative emotions and feelings out, the negativity comes back to them and make them even more negative.

Knowing all that, what should you do? The first rule is to be positive—no matter what!

Stay positive at all times. Eventually the positive energy you throw out into the world will come back to reward you. But always remember to be patient. The universe has a lot of people to take care of, so it might take longer than you expect. It's all about divine timing. Your turn will come—you just have to keep at it, keep throwing the positive out there. And enjoy yourself and your journey in the meantime.

Impatience is also a negative energy that will interfere with your efforts to be positive. Patience is a positive force that will keep driving and steering your efforts to be positive towards happiness.

But what can you do to keep your positive energy and spirits up while waiting for the energy of the world and universe to reward you? You can involve yourself in positive activities, such as reading a book or taking a course that interests you.

Make sure you always do something constructive to make the most out of each and every moment you have in your life. But also remember that being kind to yourself means taking time out to relax and wind down.

It's also very important to have goals in life. Just don't wait around expecting everything to be handed to you on a silver platter one day. And don't believe that once you have reached your goal you will be happy. Believing this will never make you happy because all you will ever do is chase happiness in vain. You must be happy with what you have *now!* Don't worry about what you will have some time in the future. Being happy now is the only way to be truly happy. Appreciate everything you have and appreciate everything that comes to you as it comes.

We are often happiest when we are least preoccupied with a quest for happiness. There is nothing you can do or accomplish that can make you happy or satisfied.

The secret to life is just *being, living,* and *enjoying!*

Let go of expectations—you only set yourself up for disappointment if they don't happen.

Gigi G.

Another secret to true happiness is to realise you and your life are not another's. They are yours. They are unique! So why try to be like others or have what others have? Your unique existence is made to fit *you*. What others have or do will not necessarily work for you.

Part of your journey towards happiness is being satisfied with yourself and your unique life (and accepting and being happy with the present as it exists for you). That doesn't mean you have to let go of your dreams—your dreams can give you direction in life. They are what you can travel towards. But dreams are very different from expectations. Expectations arise from what you think you should have in reward for what you do (based on what others have and do). They involve comparing yourself to others—that is, trying not to be you. That's silly!

Every person should be his or her own unique self—including you. How boring would this world be if everyone was the same? You are *you,* and you should be proud of that!

Dreams, however, are your own personalised road map to your life. They give your life direction so you don't wander or travel along aimlessly. You don't achieve anything without knowing what direction you want to travel in.

Be more like a child. Don't be bothered with what is going to happen when you reach the corner—or what will happen next week or next year. Be intrigued by your present situation.

Seek beauty and interest in every moment. In this way, you will always be happy and satisfied. The child exists in all of us. Just look within yourself and you will find your inner child.

Forgiveness Is a Healing Gift You Give Yourself!

We all have the choice to forgive. Forgiveness of others relieves the burdens of the hurt, anger, and pain you hold onto when you refuse to forgive someone for something they did.

Always remember that the negative feelings and emotions you harbour against others (by not forgiving them) are hurting you; burdening you. You might think that it hurts the other person—and it might—but the most important thing to understand is that it actually hurts you the most!

Why do that to yourself? No one could possibly be worth hurting yourself in that way.

The good news is that it's never too late to start forgiving. Because you ultimately control your life and how you live it, you can get rid of those negative feelings and emotions attached to that lack of forgiveness and give yourself a break (and a chance to be happy and positive). How? That's the easy part—by letting go of them and forgiving the people who created them inside of you in the first place. Any negative emotions you have attached to whatever it was they did or said to hurt you will become a part of your past. There, it can't hurt you or make you feel bad anymore.

You know what else your act of forgiveness does for you? It also gives others the freedom to live life and resolve all their own behaviours, feelings, and consequences.

"How does that help me?" you ask. By forgiving, you have created healing in those around you. That healing surrounds you and helps lead you towards your ultimate goal of happiness and self-fulfilment. That's how it helps you!

But remember that you can't change others or make them behave a certain way. But you can choose how you deal with the feelings attached to what they say or do—and that is true freedom.

But first—before you can give yourself the gift of forgiveness—you must look within yourself and ask who you blame for your present state of mind and circumstances. Turn back to your first days on this Earth.

Humans characteristically blame others for their misery in life before taking responsibility for their lives. You must always remember that the actions of others are merely circumstances in your life. The only reason you may be miserable as a result (and why you might blame others for your miseries) is because of the way you have reacted to the experience.

The way that you deal with another's actions is vital to how you develop. If you treat negative experiences arising from the actions of others as challenges brought into your life to strengthen your character and mould you, you will never blame others for your life. There will be no reason to forgive anyone—you will be living in a healthy and positive environment, taking responsibility for your own happiness.

But harbouring anger and not taking control of your power to forgive will only make your entire state of happiness dependent on the actions of others. Your life will be easily manipulated by others, and you will never have a chance to be truly happy.

That is why forgiveness is essential. It empowers you to make your life a happy one, a care-free one. You will be in charge! And once you are in charge, you can choose how you live your life. The key is to forgive—let go. Take back control of your life and how you view it … and live it!

Change the Label!

The concept in this chapter is all about understanding what labels you have placed on your feelings and experiences to date. It is all about learning to create new and more positive labels for them.

The first step to doing this is to get in touch with your own feelings about those events in your life that you feel have held you back. Take a pen and notepad and write down everything you feel at the moment. Write down everything you feel about each aspect of your life, both in the past and the present.

Access your old feelings and figure out where they came from. What event or events do you think you developed those feelings from? Write down a list of the events that you think you have had problems overcoming in the past (or even now), and write down the feelings you attach to each of those events.

Gigi G.

Take your time to complete this list because you will be accessing a vast amount of emotion, and that doesn't take five minutes to do. You must concentrate on this exercise.

When you decide that you have exhausted your resources, take a good look at what you have written down. Tick all the negative feelings that you have written down.

Can you see them? Now it is time to challenge each one.

Only concentrate on one feeling or emotion at any one moment. Notice and understand the connections between the negative experiences and the negative emotions you still carry around with you today. Understanding the reasons for your feelings is one of the keys to mastering your own life.

Freedom lies in understanding all your feelings and where they came from (and in your ability to learn from and apply that knowledge that comes from understanding where they came from).

Now get another piece of paper and write down the events again. This time, don't write down the negative emotions you attached to them.

Instead, write down all the things you learned from each of those events. What did those events teach you? What did you learn about yourself? How can you use that lesson in your life now? How could you use what you have learned to help others? How can that lesson help you in the future to have a more positive life?

This new list is the start of your new and more positive process of changing your labels. This is what you need to keep going.

Change the negative ways you see your experiences in life and start giving them more positive labels that are more about growth and learning from those experiences. After all, growth and learning are positive things that will move your life forward.

Keep using the list if you have to. Over time, you will be able to make those lists in your head as the experiences present themselves to you.

Learn to allow life to happen and ask yourself: *What can I learn from this experience that will make my life better?*

What can I take with me from this experience that will shape me and my life in a more positive way?

It is such a simple thing, but the labels you attach to your experiences in life will mould who you become and how you actually experience and feel about your life.

Start ripping those old labels off, and get started with your new ones! There's no time like the present to start.

Sweep away the Anger!

Anger can span a variety of emotions: minor irritation, frustration, annoyance, uncontrollable rage, disappointment, resentment, or hurt.

Everyone feels anger sometimes, but not everyone expresses it. It is harmful to hold such an emotion; however, it is also harmful to express it in a rage. So how do you deal with it in a healthy way? First you have to ask yourself, "Why do I feel this way?" You've got to get to the nub of it and understand why it is you are upset.

Also, you have to know and understand how it affects you physically and psychologically. Do you feel dizzy? Do you lose your breath? Do you become hot, have palpitations, become flustered? Do you become depressed or high strung afterwards? Are there any other symptoms? You've got to write down (or mentally list) how you physically feel during and after a bout of anger. You've got to learn how to direct your anger in a way that is not going to hurt yourself or others. You've got to learn how to take the fire out of it.

If you are coming home from a difficult day at work and you are irritated, blowing up at your family because dinner is not ready (or any other event) would be an inappropriate expression of anger. Wouldn't you agree?

Expressing anger is a natural and healthy response. That is, it is necessary to stay healthy and balanced. But learning how you express or get rid of it in a healthy way is the key.

Specificity is a good measure of appropriate anger. If you can identify the specific reason why you feel a certain way, you can deal with it.

More often than not, it is not what others do or say, but your reaction to them that is the reason for your expression of anger. I have also realised that, in my own life, anger usually starts long before the event or actions occur. In my experience, anger stems from a negative emotion one has held onto for years, which hasn't been dealt with or forgiven. The negative emotion gets bigger and bigger as time goes by, and it becomes so big that it can only express itself as anger.

Gigi G.

When you are trying to identify what it is that made you feel angry, you more often than not need to go much further to identify when the anger started. You need to figure out which negative emotion attached to which event and allowed it to grow into this larger and more volatile emotion.

By engaging in this investigative process, you can get to the root of the emotion and question it, relabel it, deal with it, and let it go. If you can do this, there is no negative emotion left—nothing to get all worked up about.

What you will be left with is your reactions to the actual situations that present themselves to you (rather than exploding from a place that is rooted in the past and has been boiling and waiting to explode all this time).

After you have dealt with the reason you have been boiling all of these years—using all the tools you have learned so far—you need to learn how to express and deal with any anger you feel that actually relates to the situation.

How to express any anger in a healthy and productive way

Just do these exercises whenever you feel that you are getting angry, and your ability to deal with anger will improve.

Take a deep breath and remember your anger is just your reaction to something that has happened. Knowing this, calmly tell a friend (or even the person you're angry with) that you are experiencing anger. Dig deep within yourself to share with that person the thing or incident that made you feel that way. Remember the anger you are experiencing is only your reaction to the situation. It arises because that is how you have allowed yourself to react in that situation.

By sharing what exactly caused your anger to arise, you will be able to understand how you are wired. Understanding this is crucial because, once you know how you are wired to react, you can work on rewiring yourself not to react that way.

Release your anger at an appropriate time and in an appropriate situation. Find vehicles for release so you can wait until a time that you consider appropriate before expressing anger. Usually, by the time you reach your vehicle of release, you will find that much of your anger has gone away. The issue does not seem as infuriating. You will have calmed down and acquired the ability to look back on the situation rationally.

Learn to identify with your anger as a natural and major part of growing up and the healing process. Becoming stuck with or dwelling upon anger can result in depression, loneliness, confusion, and frustration. Sustained anger can develop into generalised rage that can be detrimental to your well-being.

Gigi G.

Allow yourself to feel the emotions, but recognise that they are only emotions—a natural process in your life journey. Allow these processes to occur and learn from them. Learn how to cope with those processes if they occur again in the future.

Allow yourself to remove the feeling from your anger so you can diffuse the emotion, actually deal with it, and then let it go.

Avoid becoming a people pleaser. Avoid disguising your anger by clenching your teeth or holding it all in. In this way, the anger transforms into physical complaints such as headaches, backaches, etc. It only ends up hurting you.

Breathe! Always remember to breathe! When you feel angry, start breathing deeply. Each time you breathe out, let a little of the anger be taken away with your breath. Eventually, you will be left with the situation you need to attend to, learn from, and deal with (without all the anger attached to it). By removing the feelings attached to the situation, you are better able to calmly deal with it and talk it through with others.

When you talk through it calmly, there is a much better chance of it getting resolved and you being able to move past it and leave it in the past.

The Glass IS Full

After you are done dealing with it (without the emotion attached), appreciate yourself for being honest and direct. Congratulate yourself for being able to accomplish the task without the emotion attached. Always appreciate and congratulate yourself. This is part of appreciating who you are, which is an essential part of being able to enjoy and appreciate your life.

Take Responsibility for Your Existence—Take Charge!

You alone have the power to change your own life. Blaming others for your hurt only reinforces the feeling of lack of control in your life. You must forgive and forget.

Let go of the blame and allow yourself to finally take responsibility for your life and actions. This may seem like a very difficult task at first, but once you have taken control, you will find that you can make good things happen for yourself.

Dwelling on the past is not constructive. Instead, concentrate on taking control of what you are doing now. This is another recurrent theme of my philosophy:

Live your life in the now!

Take charge of the present!

To be free of negative energy, you must detach yourself from the behaviour of others. Other people will hurt you if you allow them to, which then feeds them with the power to manipulate you. You will find yourself trapped in someone else's life, neglecting your own.

Realise that you have power, and that the power is not in the manipulation of others, but in the transformation of yourself into a happy person. That is all that matters in this life. The sooner you accept this, the sooner you will be able to lead a happy life.

Goodbye, Guilt!

In my experience, guilt comes from holding anger in and turning it against yourself. It arises when you wallow in the negative feelings as a form of self-punishment. I also know it can happen when you have difficulties directing anger appropriately—you direct it at yourself.

Looked at simply, guilt is just another negative energy that keeps those negative experiences coming back into your life. It functions as a negativity magnet until you can let it go and establish a truly positive attitude.

You have to sit down (yes, again!) and write down those things that you feel guilty about. Ask yourself—and be completely honest with yourself—"What am I angry at myself about? What things am I feeling guilty about?"

Do you feel guilty for having that chocolate bar the other day? Do you feel guilty for an indulgence you allowed yourself recently? Do you feel guilty for something you said or did to someone recently?

The first thing to recognise is that things you might feel guilty about are in the past. Am I right? I mean, they have already happened, haven't they? This means we need to go back to the lesson of letting go. You need to resolve your feelings attached to the past so you can let go of them with love and acceptance.

Part of the process of acceptance requires confronting your feelings head-on and understanding that holding onto guilt will only end up making you sick.

Another part of the process of acceptance is understanding and accepting that what has happened is in the past—and you can't change the past. Accept this with love and peace. There is no point fighting this because there is nothing you can do about what is in the past. For that reason, accepting it with love and peace is the best option. And then accept that whatever happened has happened for a reason—whether you can see that reason now or not, you simply have to trust that it has happened for a reason.

There is reason and purpose behind everything!

Now, if you've got feelings of guilt attached to that event in the past, you need to write down what exactly gave rise to those feelings.

What precisely do you feel guilty about? Face it head-on!

It might be hard to go through this process. You might feel sick or cry. But you have to do it for your own sake. You have to clean this guilt cupboard out—otherwise, it is just going to get mouldy and start making you sick!

Once you have identified the precise things you feel guilty about, it is time to apologise (if there is another person involved). If the person is no longer alive, speak to that person's spirit or soul and ask for forgiveness. Let go of the pain you have been holding onto by starting with this task. And then you have to forgive yourself!

Remember forgiveness is a gift you give to yourself.

Unless you forgive yourself, it doesn't matter who forgives you.

So forgiving yourself and accepting that you are only human will allow you to come to terms with what you have done. Forgiving yourself will also allow you to finally take the negative label off that event and allow you to place a new label on it—a more positive one. This new label can be one that defines the positives associated with that event. For example, the lesson you learned from that event is a new and more positive label that you can attach to that event.

As a part of attaching a new label for that event, you have to get used to going through the process of accepting the following: it is what it is; the past is in the past; you are human and must live life without regret; and you must always look for the positive in all things past to be able to live in the now with peace and happiness.

But always remember everything that you do must come from a place of great self-worth. If you feel you are worthy of forgiveness, then the act of forgiving yourself will be a much easier process.

Once you have done all these things, you are free to let go of the guilt attached to those actions in the past (with love and acceptance and peace) and finally leave them in the past for good.

> **Do what you can to clean out the past**
> **and make the now different**
> **so that the future can follow suit.**

You Matter!

•

Have you ever found yourself making compromises for others and hurting inside as a result? Sometimes those compromises are about compromising who you are as a person. I am not talking about making compromises in situations, I'm talking about changing who you are.

For example, have you been quiet around people because your partner doesn't like the way you talk or how loud your voice is? Have you avoided going out for lunch with friends because your partner doesn't like you going out without those friends? Have you been prevented from doing the things that make you truly happy because someone else stops you? If so, have you asked yourself, "What am I doing with this person in the first place?"

Why sacrifice being who you are to be in a relationship with someone? If there is no trust now, it's never going to change.

Many people find themselves stuck in jobs or relationships or situations that make them miserable. They allow people to walk all over them at the expense of their own happiness. But why? There is no reason why you should allow this to happen.

It's one thing to make compromises in situations, for example, for the better good of the family—but not when that compromise means you have to compromise yourself as a person (and sacrifice your happiness in the process).

Acknowledge your feelings, don't push them to the side completely, and allow yourself to truly accept that your feelings, your life, and your happiness do matter. You are important because you are the centre of your life—the key actor in your own journey.

Be true to your own needs. By addressing your own needs, the way others feel and act around you will naturally fall into place. Surround yourself with people who accept you for who you are. Strive to meet your own needs as often as you can and be honest with yourself.

Part of your happiness in life might come from making others happy—and that is perfectly all right ... as long as you are being true to yourself. I know that part of what makes me truly happy is to see my husband and children truly happy. Some of my life is focused on making sure their needs are met because part of what makes me happy is their happiness.

Gigi G.

Ask yourself the following:

1. What do I want from my life?

2. What makes me truly happy in terms of emotional things, things I can't buy?

3. How can I achieve the emotional happiness that I desire?

4. What obstacles exist preventing me from achieving that state of happiness I desire?

5. Who or what placed them there? Me, others, or certain situations?

6. Why should I wait for a crisis or a state of desperation or illness to force me to take action?

7. Where do I go from here?

Your journey is yours alone!

Remember that no one owns you but yourself. Those around you are fortunate to have you in their lives, and you are fortunate to have those you care about and love in yours. We are all sharing our journeys with each other, but we are each the central actor in our own journey.

You owe it to yourself to be honest and loyal to yourself. Only *you* can really be true to yourself. Only *you* can take charge and control your life.

Your journey in this life is a road to dream fulfilment. Always remember that! Be responsible to and for yourself—you matter in your own life journey.

You need to accept that you owe it to yourself to be kind to yourself and think positively—no matter how negative things might seem at the time. You owe it to yourself to take care of yourself and to speak and act kindly to yourself. You should not criticise every aspect of yourself or blame others around you for how you feel. Give yourself love and appreciate it.

You deserve your own love and respect because you matter. Always remember this!

Say "Sayonara" to Shame

What is shame? "Isn't it the same as guilt?" some of you ask. Guilt is not the same as shame. Guilt is a specific emotion attached to something you have done or said to yourself or others.

Shame seems to come from feelings of low self-worth. It shows up when you are not feeling good enough as a result of something that has happened.

The trick to dealing with feelings of low self-worth is to identify where they came from, use the skill of forgiveness that you have learned (forgiving the person involved with the event and forgiving yourself for holding onto it for so long), and let go of the event. Only then can you challenge the feeling that arose from that event with something positive. You can seek the positive in the event and replace the label you have placed on the event with something positive.

For example, if you feel unattractive, ask yourself what started that feeling. Where did it come from? How long have you felt that way? Did someone say something to you, which you held onto? Did something happen to you that led you to feel that way?

Once you have identified what it was that started this negative feeling, you can face it, forgive those involved, and start relabeling it.

Remember my story about my ballet instructor. When I was eight, she told me I was ugly in front of my whole ballet class. For years, I let this affect me. I looked at myself as though I were ugly, and I felt ashamed of myself. Why? Why did I allow that person to have so much power over my life and how I viewed myself? I guess I was young and didn't know any better. But as I became an adult and looked back on all the years I allowed her comment to affect me, I realised I had complete control over how I reacted to the comment. I had the control to hold onto it or let it go with love and peace—to treat it as just another lesson or experience in my life that made me who I am today.

I chose to forgive her. I understood that she knew no better, that she did not have the good fortune to know the true meaning of kindness to others and herself. I then forgave myself for allowing the comment to affect me for so many years. I accepted and understood that I didn't know any better, that I didn't have the tools to let go of it and deal with it in a more positive way.

Gigi G.

When I finally knew and understood that I had a choice, I exercised that choice. I forgave her, I forgave myself, I let go of the comment, I left it in the past where it belonged, and I relabelled it. I considered it to be a life experience that taught me to be unaffected by the negative behaviour of others. After all, the behaviour of others is simply their behaviour, coming from their own experiences and insecurities. And then I turned my feeling about this comment into more positive ones. I now look at myself and see my inner beauty. I see that there is no need to feel shame about anything because shame holds me back from being happy. Shame is connected to the past—where the past should remain—and all I need to worry about is enjoying the present and being grateful for the chance to make my present and future better.

You can do this too. Look at yourself in the mirror, deep into your eyes, and see the beautiful person within you. Look into your soul. Say to yourself, "I am beautiful" and, "I am worthy of my own love and appreciation." There is nothing to be ashamed about. All you have to do is make peace with whatever has made you feel that way and move away from it. You need to realise there is no need or purpose to holding onto it any more. It doesn't serve you; it holds you back from being happy.

Sometimes, people feel shame for things others do or say—but why? To what end? Again it is just a negative emotion that holds you back from being and feeling happy.

If someone has done something to make you feel that emotion, you have to accept that that person is only human. And you also need to forgive that person—acknowledge he or she is just a person who has a journey of his or her own to lead. That which is inside that person is what makes him or her valuable (not what the person does). Also remember that *you* are only human and can be forgiven for allowing yourself to feel shame as a result of another's actions. Apologise to yourself for allowing this feeling to develop, reconcile yourself with the actions or words of that other person, and don't worry yourself with trying to figure out why. It happened—just accept that fact.

Finally, look for the lesson in the actions or words, let go of incident, and move on (taking with you the lessons that you have learned from it).

It's exactly like picking yourself up, brushing yourself off, learning the lesson, and moving on. It is that simple!

Be confident in who you are, be proud of who you are within yourself, and take the lessons with you like souvenirs from your journey. That way, you can look back on them and use them to move forward positively in your life.

Living Positively

Being happy is all about living each moment of your life in a positive way. You should be positive, exhibit positive energy, do positive things, and use your time to grow. See the world with positive eyes!

The more you focus on the positive in your life, the more you will be and feel positive.

One way to get this process started—apart from applying all the tools you have learned so far on your journey with me—is to take a sheet of paper and write down all your positive short-term and long-term goals. Then make a true commitment within yourself to keep moving towards them. Know that you deserve to reach them, that you are worthy of all the good this world has to offer.

Make sure that every moment you are doing something constructive and positive and moving towards your goals. But always remember to be happy in the moment and appreciate each minute of your journey towards each of those goals.

The goals might change as time passes. You might change them because your appreciation of each day gives you a different perspective about your life. You might find yourself realising that what makes you truly happy is something completely different from what you thought it would be in your initial list of goals.

There are many ways you can live your life positively.

One thing you can do is make sure you do not have too much "un-utilised" time on your hands. What do I mean by *un-utilised?* I mean it is best to use your time in positive ways every day—even if that results in you relaxing in your garden, reading a book, sinking yourself into your work, going for a walk, or taking a good siesta. Choose something that will make you feel happy and give you some feelings of joy in your life. But remember that creating feelings of joy is a skill.

Also, learn to appreciate all the beauty around you, and then you can live positively and do things with a positive mind. Read a spiritually uplifting book—keeping the mind working is essential to your overall well-being. But always remember to take everything in moderation. Also make time for relaxation—anything that will refocus your mind and re-energise you (physically or emotionally or spiritually).

Learn to keep company with positive people. People who mainly carry around negative energy will reflect their negative energies onto you and drain your positive energy resources. Once you capture their negative energies within your magnetic field, the energies will magnify like a pebble dropping into a pool of water (creating larger ripples, eventually disturbing the whole pattern of calmness that once existed).

Join a health club or take part in some alternative form of exercise to aid you in the release of negative energies that build up throughout your day. You must realise, however, that insight and disclosure of negative feelings will not automatically release you from your depression.

You must also let go of any expectations of how your life should have been and should be. Such expectations make present moments in your life appear inadequate and outside of your control. Again, we touch on the fundamental principle of the universe: always make the best of the present moments in your life; separate yourself from making comparisons of what you should have done and had with what you did and do possess.

Another technique for releasing yourself from negative energy and living positively is to restrain yourself from being too emotionally expressive when releasing your negative emotions. Excess expressive behaviour leads to excess emotionality, and subsequently, your coping mechanisms will suffer. You may also find yourself dwelling on expressions of negative emotions as a result.

A good idea is to take your emotions and refocus them. Write a poem, compose a song, start some form of exercise, or do any other form of constructive energy release. Yoga, t'ai chi, or deep-breathing exercises are good forms of refocusing yourself.

How about a good massage? I have a deep muscle massage once every two to three weeks, which re-energises me. The feeling is akin to having your car battery replaced—I feel so revitalised and refreshed. I have recommended this technique to many others, and everyone who has taken my advice has experienced the same benefits.

Another technique is to detach yourself for a moment from your present state of mind and search for a reason why your depression and anger have developed. Search for the source—for example, the loss of a loved one, suppression of your emotions during childhood, embarrassing moments in your childhood, etc. What happened to you, especially when you were young, that could have contributed to the way you think and feel about yourself? How did you feel at the time, and how do you feel about it now? Write everything that comes to your mind; leave nothing unexpressed.

Now observe each experience and related feeling. By writing everything down, you are gaining insight into your depression. Next, you must realise that these situations became blown out of proportion, and they should have been confronted and released long ago. Next, treat each situation as a valuable lesson in your life that has contributed to your strength as a human being. Detach yourself from your past and make room for the present. Open yourself to the wealth of experiences around you in this lifetime—flourish from them. Richness of experience and opening your eyes to all views of the universe is a certain method to bypass the road to depression.

Always remember that, among the experiences that you once might have labelled as "bad" in your life, there is always something good and positive to draw from them—you've just got to remind yourself that the good and positive are *always* there.

Consider a dark, cloudy day. Even the dark clouds will begin to break up and allow the sun to shine through every now and again. Life is the same.

Be committed to freeing yourself of emotional and negative baggage from your past, so you can free yourself and move forward with new and more positive labels, feelings and emotions. This is the only way you can truly live positively and be happy.

Understand your feelings and transform them into positive experiences, positive feelings, and positive statements about yourself. By doing this, you will experience self-mastery, independence, and freedom.

Go for it!

Letting Go of Desires for Revenge

Seeking revenge for past wrongs will only end up hurting you. You will never be free of negativity if you burden yourself with the goal of revenge. Working towards such a negative goal only keeps you tied to a path of negativity. Nothing will ever work out for you because your mind, heart, and soul are buried in and focused on negative energy.

It's like I said before: forgiveness is a gift you give to yourself. Even when you forgive others, you are giving a gift to yourself—the gift of letting go of the past and the negative feelings attached to it and others.

The other thing you should always remember is that there is no such thing as a negative experience—it is simply an experience. It only becomes a negative experience when you label it as one, when you see it as one.

If you take that label away and see it for what it is (and accept that it is a thing of the past), you can relabel that experience with a positive label. Remember there is always a lesson to be learned from an experience because it is simply that—an experience in your life from which you can learn and grow. This fact in itself is a positive thing because growth is positive, learning is positive.

So, rip that angry and negative label off whatever someone has done—rip off that negative label you have attached to that person—and understand and accept that what that person has done is contributing to your learning and growth. You can live in the now with that lesson in mind and work towards the future with that lesson tucked under your belt.

That lesson or that experience has probably made you wiser. Am I right? That lesson or experience has probably made you a little tougher—yes? That lesson or experience has probably taught you something about yourself—yes? All of those things are positives because you can take them with you as tools in your belt for the now and the future.

So, forgive the person attached to that event—the person you have been angry at—because that person has taught you something. This is your path. Just accept it, move on, and take with you the positives you've acquired.

Gigi G.

Allow the pain and anger to dissolve. Allow yourself to set and pursue positive goals with your tools from that event. As a result, your life will transform into a pool of positive energy. This positive energy will multiply and come back to you. So, always make sure that this energy is positive.

Relax!

The key to ultimate happiness is a fruitful combination of letting go of fear and negativity, acceptance, and relaxation.

There are many different ways you can relax: focused breathing, relaxing and calming self-talk, exercise, yoga, Pilates, walking, meditation, writing, singing … and the list goes on. I mainly use writing, Pilates, singing, listening to music, and focused breathing.

With focused breathing, you can really get to a place where your mind is cleared and centred—a neutral emotional place, a place where you can just exist, a place where your body and mind hold onto nothing. This is a great place to be because, out of this place, comes clarity—a clear and unemotional state of mind. Because of this, your body will follow suit and relax. It will be unburdened by any worries or negativity attached to the distant or not so distant events that have past.

Gigi G.

When you are breathing, focus on something neutral. I always focus on what I have heard people call the third eye. I call it my mind's eye, which I visualise between my two seeing eyes, on the bridge of my nose. You've probably heard others call it the mind's eye, too. I find it effective because it focuses me on a place which is within me but completely neutral. This place might work for you, but if you have some other focus point that gives you the same neutrality, use that. There are no rules to life, just what works for you!

In that neutral place—with that focus—you will be able to think of nothing but your focus on the silence, calm, and peace of that place. The aim is to focus on your breathing exclusively—the slow pace of it, the peacefulness and calmness of it.

"So how do I do it?" you ask.

One way is to sit down with your back straight (but supported and comfortable) and rest your hands by your side with your palms facing upward and your feet comfortably flat on the ground. Close your eyes and take a slow, deep breath to a *slow* count of eight. Count in your mind as follows: "One, two, three, four, five, six, seven, eight." Do this at a good, steady pace. Hold for a second at the end of your count, and then breathe out to a slow count of eight.

Repeat this process while staying focused on your breathing at all times. Just allow external distractions (and any distracting thoughts) to be taken away by the outward breath. Visualise and feel all the negative energy travel out of you with the breath and dissipate into the atmosphere. With each breath you take in, visualise a brilliant, white, and clean ray of light coming into your body with your breath. Feel the warmth of it spread throughout your body. Repeat this entire process for as long as you see fit.

When you feel relaxed and centred and calm—and you feel the warmth and boost of the positive energy you have been breathing in (in the form of the white light)—you have reached your place of calmness and neutrality. Stay in that state for as long as you are able to. Allow the peace to fill you up. This is a state in which you can accept life and what it has to offer you in terms of experiences. This is a state in which you can let go of all the negative energies you have held onto. This is a state in which you can allow the past to be carried away and replaced by calmness and peace. With this state of mind—a place of Zen—you are able to see the world in a better light (from a positive mindset).

Just make sure that you are uninterrupted during your breathing session. (Hint: disconnect the phone or put it on silent and ask people not to disturb you.)

Gigi G.

I find that ten minutes is a good minimum amount of time to reap the benefits. But I always also say that if you can fit any amount in—wherever you can—the benefits will accrue like money in a piggy bank. Remember it's not about how fast you get there; it's about getting there and enjoying the journey.

When you are finished counting, don't just jump up and start going about your business as per usual. Make sure you return from your journey of relaxation gradually. Allow yourself to become slowly aware of your surroundings. Return to your fully conscious state bit by bit with each breath in and each breath out (but keep that relaxed mindset at the same time).

Gradually, bring your breathing pace back to a more normal one. Only move from your position when you are completely aware of yourself and your surroundings. You can still be relaxed—just make sure you are completely aware, not half-asleep.

This entire exercise is a simple form of meditation. In times of stress, you can use focused breathing to centre yourself and neutralise your emotions. That way you will be able to make more objective decisions.

Sometimes, however, there is no time or opportunity to take up the seated position. It doesn't matter! You can do it anywhere and any time! You can do some focused breathing while you're walking to work, for example. It's just a matter of refocusing, clearing the mind, relaxing, letting go, and preparing your mind to be filled with positive thoughts and emotions.

Of course, it's better if you can have some actual peace and quiet. But if you can master doing it while you are walking amid the hustle and bustle, that's even better. If you can do it literally anywhere at any time, you have a greater chance of success at clearing yourself out and relaxing wherever you are. What a great skill to have—practise it wherever you are!

Still, I do suggest having your first go at it in a quiet place where you can really focus and practise at it without distractions.

Another technique I use to relax and let go is self-talk. If you're feeling stressed or anxious, it is a good idea to adopt relaxing and calming self-talk. Just say to yourself assertively (but calmly), "Relax." Now say to yourself ten times slowly, "I feel relaxed." Now say, "I feel calm and happy" ten times. Repeat this exercise until you feel more relaxed and focused.

When using self-talk, you can expand your statements to other positive affirmations to make you relax. The list of statements is endless. Use statements that are appropriate for your circumstances—but make sure that they are purely positive in character. Make sure that your statements are free of words such as *don't, won't, can't,* or any other negative verbs. Those words will cause you to concentrate on the activity you are not supposed to be doing. For example, I don't want you to think about a purple elephant. I guarantee that the first thing you did was think of one, right? You thought about the purple elephant because I drew your attention to it. The very same principle applies to statements to yourself such as, "Don't feel anxious" or "I won't feel anxious." You will have drawn your attention to the feeling of anxiety—so, you will feel anxious. This applies to all negative statements. So, make sure that you tell yourself to do or be positive things—or feel positive emotions—rather than tell yourself not to feel negative emotions or think negative thoughts.

If you ever feel tense, say your positive statements that emphasise feeling relaxed and calm ten times. Try saying, "I am calm," "I am relaxed." If you feel unhappy, try saying, "I am happy," "I am full of joy and happiness," "I feel the warmth of happiness." If you are feeling unattractive say, "I am beautiful inside and out," "I am a beautiful person," and "I am attractive in my very own special and unique way."

There are so many ways of letting go of negative emotions—all you have to do is find and use the positive ways that work for you.

Life Is Like a Big Bowl of Soup!

"What does she mean now?" some of you say. Think about it. Let's see if you can figure it out after having come this far on your journey with me. Why don't you write down what you think I mean (in light of the lessons you have learned so far). Try to see the analogy between life and a good bowl of soup.

Have you done that? Now see if you're right.

I find the art of using analogies really does help make sense of life. Let's have a look at the bowl of soup.

Why did I use soup as an example?

Downstairs from my workplace is a wonderful cafe and restaurant. Marco is the owner. Marco's dad makes the best chicken and mixed vegetable soup. I go crazy and buy a huge tub of it for

Gigi G.

my family every time he makes it, and my five year old loves it. She even made a video message for Marco's dad that she gave me to show him. In it, she says how much she loves his soup.

So what is it about this soup that is like life? What makes it such a success? If you think about it, what is a soup made of? Water perhaps? Water gives it the flow it needs. Life needs flow. When you pour it, it just flows in whichever way you direct it. You can do that with your life—take control and direct it. It will just flow if all is as you allow it to be. So life is like soup in that sense.

You've got to work at it sometimes to get the right consistency, but learning from recipes or techniques that didn't quite get you there in the past will help you each time you have another go at getting it right. Just like life, right?

In this soup, there are also vegetables—a whole lot of different vegetables. Each vegetable is lovely and tasty on its own, but when thrown together, they can present a symphony of wonderful flavours. You've got to keep trying different groups of vegetables in this soup each time you make it to figure out what vegetables give it the flavour that you want. Again, just like life—you've got to try different things in life and allow the experiences to happen so you can take from those experiences the lessons that will work for you now and in the future. The lessons are your ingredients. Choose the good ones to equip yourself to make your life's soup a tasty one.

The ingredients can also give the soup a wonderful colour, depending on which ones you use. Just like life, there are so many experiences in our lives, which are the ingredients that mould us into who we are and where we go in life. If we use the ingredients that work best, the next time we make the soup, it will taste even better and look even more vibrant.

It's the same with life: if you take the good ingredients and lessons from the experiences in your life, carry them with you, and apply them to your life as you live it, your life can only get better and better. It will become filled with many different colours!

And the *pièce de résistance* is the chicken breast or tenderloins. The fat is trimmed off the meat, and you are left with the best, healthiest, and tastiest part. That is another secret to a good life—making sure you take the best of what presents itself to you in life. Seek out the best aspect of a situation you find yourself in—no matter how grey the situation might initially seem. If you take out of every situation in life the best parts (and carry those best parts with you into your daily life), your life can only get better.

Cut away all the unhealthy bits—such as the negative energies—just like you would cut the fat off the chicken. That is a recipe for a healthy life.

Gigi G.

Feed your soul just as you would feed your stomach with soup. The more positivity you feed your soul, the better you are going to feel (and the more energy you are going to have)—just like eating a healthy bowl of soup!

Whenever you are in a challenging situation, perhaps you can remind yourself of the soup.

If you arm yourself with all the best ingredients on offer in your life and throw them all in to the big cooking pot that is your life, it can only turn out great.

Remember that life is just like that big bowl of soup!

Smile and the Whole World Will Smile with You

It's amazing how a smile can bring so much happiness to your life. Smiling will make you feel good and positive, and flashing smiles at everyone around you will usually result in more smiles.

Smiles are like boomerangs; when you throw one out, it eventually comes back to you. It's the same with any other emotion you throw out there. For example, if you throw aggression out, it will come back to you somehow (with the same force … or more).

Smiles move back and forth between people with ease, and they magnify positivity within and around you. But always remember that it may not return to you immediately—that's normal. Some people may not as receptive to the positive emotions around them because they are so burdened with negativity themselves.

Gigi G.

That's why it's important to do your best to keep company with positive people. However, always remember that the smile and positivity that it generates will return to you in time—usually when you need it the most.

Smile and the whole world will smile with you.

Frown and you will frown alone!

One way of staying positive is to steer clear of the frowners. The negative energy the frowners throw out with their frowns will bounce off you, and you will end up sending that energy out to others. This will magnify the negativity within and around you. People will end up wanting to steer clear of you, and you may find yourself drowning in that misery alone!

Think carefully for a moment. Who would you rather spend time with, someone who is happy and positive about life or someone who is depressed, frowning, and complaining about life? I know what my choice would be.

Another way to deal with the frowners is to give them a smile. I often find when I am dealing with someone who is affected by a negative emotion that it is best to just respond with a smile. It's best to understand that it is not my problem. Recognising a person is having difficulty with an issue is very important because you don't take it on as your own problem. You simply recognise it as that person's problem, and you try to shield yourself by throwing a smile and positive energy back at them. By doing this, you are not giving their negativity power. Instead, you are diffusing it. This is kind of like the flow of a gentle stream of water on a fire or the beautiful warmth of the sun on ice.

The more you deal with those around you in a positive way—with a gentle, genuine smile and the belief that you can make a difference by being positive—you will be amazed how much more positive your experiences in life will be. Just keep at it and trust in the power of the positive energy in your smile. In short, keep smiling!

Be Kind to Yourself and to Others

I have always thought to myself, *If each person in this world performed one act of kindness towards another person each day, the world would be so amazing.* It would hit the world like a wave—from one person to the next—and there would be no reason for war. You each have the power in your hands to start this wave on its journey.

Every day, when you get up, make a promise to yourself that you will be kind not only to yourself, but also to at least one person that day. You will not only feel great when you are kind to others, but also the feeling will multiply and come back to you one way or another.

If each person chose to find that very small amount of time to be kind to other people around them, the world would fill up with that beautiful, kind, and loving energy. Perhaps I might be seen as a little ambitious, but think about how amazing it would be if everyone acted this way.

If you see someone having problems walking across the street, why not offer to help him or her? When you see your friends or family, tell them something positive to make them feel good. When you see your children, give them a big hug and tell them how much they are loved. When you see people who are upset, lend them your ear and comfort them. Acknowledge how they are feeling and reassure them that everything will be okay. Tell them that all they have to do is believe that life is full of lessons, and there is always something good that can come from every lesson.

When I see a homeless man sleeping on the street, I go to the corner store, buy a loaf of bread and some juice, and give it to him. That way, he has something to eat and drink for a couple of days. It might not be much, but it helps that person—even if just for a short time. That might just be the boost that man needed to get him back on the positive path in life.

Give a little of what you have to a charity each month if you can—spread the good around. Give a little of your energy each day to making someone else's life feel a little brighter. And remember to be just as kind and loving to yourself. Pat yourself on the back for those things that make you special and wonderful. Tell yourself each day that you are a wonderful and special human being (and that there is no one else exactly like you in this world). When you feel down, give yourself a lift by telling yourself about all of those positive things that make you and your life a wonder to be thankful for. Avoid criticising yourself, and always look for ways to be positive about your life. Avoid saying bad things about yourself. You would not want someone else to do that to you—why do it to yourself?

Most importantly, treat yourself and love yourself in the way you would want others to treat you and love you. Remember this each day. Send yourself a reminder each day saying, "Be kind to myself and others." It is just a matter of reminding yourself to do it for a while before it becomes a part of who you are. And as others remind themselves to do the same, the wave will grow and spread further and further. This will give the world the gift of love and kindness that is capable of creating lasting peace.

Slow Down and Enjoy the Journey

Life can get a little hectic and fast-paced at times—would you agree? There are many things going on at one time, pulling you in different directions. The secret to dealing with those situations is to accept that you can only properly deal with one issue at a time. And then you can allow your mind to focus on each issue and trust that everything will get sorted out in time.

One of the problems with our society is that we are taught to overburden ourselves with several issues at once in an effort to prove that we are superhuman and capable of handling everything without any problems. But our minds end up racing around so much that we don't have time to appreciate every aspect of what we are doing. If we're focusing on too many things at once, we're selling ourselves short.

Gigi G.

You won't be satisfied with what you do if you don't focus on enjoying every aspect of the activity. You'll find that trying to rush and do many things at once will disrupt you and your whole body. You'll most likely feel flustered and confused. You might miss a detail that is important. And you certainly won't enjoy the task because you are juggling it with so many others. You miss out on enjoying it altogether.

If you find yourself in such a situation (where you are working on or doing many things at once), stop for a moment, take a breath, and acknowledge what you are doing.

At first, you should write down what you need to achieve and the order in which things must be done. And then you can focus on the most important task first. Finish what you set out to finish, and then move on to the next task. Look at your day and see where you can realistically fit things in. If they don't need to be done urgently, see where you can squeeze them in at a later time—and make sure you set aside enough time to focus on the task and do it properly.

Diaries are actually a wonderful thing because they remind you what you need to do that day. You can organise your energy and time accordingly. Make sure to carve out some "you time" as well, though. Perhaps a fifteen minute walk to soak up some sun outside? Perhaps a little coffee break with a friend?

Perhaps putting on a favourite song and listening to it on your headphones for fifteen minutes. Just make time to slow down and regroup.

After a while, you might not need to write these things down (including your time for yourself). But I always find that, if it is in my diary, I am more likely to achieve it.

Setting goals for each task—each day—is the key!

As you work on each task, also make sure you take time to enjoy and appreciate that activity. You'll find that your efforts will be more fruitful, and you'll feel more satisfied when you are done. You'll be satisfied that you have achieved what you set out to achieve and satisfied that you took time out for yourself in the process. Success will flow to those who make the most of everything they do. That includes you!

Enjoyment of and dedication to your goals are the keys to success

A real key to success is becoming genuinely fascinated by (or interested in) the task that you are working on at any given time. It's ideal if you can derive enjoyment from the task itself and the joy of achievement that arises from it.

This dedication to the task and enjoyment of it will allow you to let go of other issues and tasks that need to be done. After all, you will have already set aside the time for those matters—you don't need to worry about them for the time being.

Devote yourself to everything that you do, and enjoy each moment that you breathe in. Feel yourself breathe in life. This will give you energy to enjoy the moment, the task at hand. And even if you are not working on anything in that moment, that breath will give you a chance to slow down and enjoy that moment.

As you breathe in slowly, imagine a bright beam of white light coming down from the darkness of our massive universe and entering you through the top of your head. Picture it filling your head, moving through your throat, passing into your lungs, coursing through your stomach and legs and toes. Your whole body should feel enlightened and light. Actually imagine each part of your body shining brightly as the light enters and moves about. When you can breathe in no more, let the breath go in a slow and controlled manner until your lungs are empty of all air. As you breathe out, allow the breath to carry away all your problems, negative emotions and preoccupations. Visualise them all being captured by a white light, and that this light is streaming out of your body … taking those problems and preoccupations away and clearing you of the negative energy attached to them. Each time you breathe out, visualise the light leaving your body with your breath—carrying your cares away with it. Repeat this exercise for at least ten minutes to make sure that all the stress you feel in your day has been released. After this exercise your mind will be completely clear and ready to focus on the task at hand.

This exercise allows you to breath in life-giving energy. Think about it! Breathing is the basis of our existence, and deep breathing enhances cell regeneration, which can help fight negative, man-made forces.

The life-giving breath allows you to focus on giving all your positive energy to the constructive activity of your choice. Feel yourself being constructive. Say to yourself, preferably aloud, "I love what I am doing," "I am enjoying life," "I am being fulfilled." Say these statements regularly during your activity and really believe in what you are saying—feel your words. You will find that your enjoyment will increase, and everything that you do will give you the greatest satisfaction. You will be happy.

Always remember to take one step at a time. Burdening yourself will only cause you to feel disharmony inside. Cramming everything is counterproductive.

Also, when you are dealing with a task, always remember that trying to climb a mountain with one footstep is impossible. When you set a big goal for yourself, divide it into a series of smaller, more easily attainable goals. Taking small steps and trying to progress another ten metres up the mountain is easier than climbing the mountain in one go without any breaks.

Gigi G.

Reward yourself each time you complete a mini-goal. For example, take a small break or put the task aside and complete a mini-goal for another major goal. In academic or work-related situations, it is best to alternate mini-goals from different activities so your mind does not become stale.

Think about picking up a 700-page book. Human nature programs you to say, "There is no way I'll be able to finish that." Then you've set up a block, and you won't be able to complete the book because you've told your subconscious not to complete it. But why? There are actually no limits to what you can do if you believe and try. All you have to do is reprogram the way you think and approach tasks—just like a computer. Just rewrite the program to be more positive and effective.

When you look at that book, learn to look at it as a series of smaller chapters. Each chapter can be read on a different day, and each chapter will open your eyes to something new. Plus, reading a chapter will take less time than you anticipate.

And each time you complete a chapter, allow yourself to feel excited about it and what you have gained from it. Why should you be excited? Because you are one chapter closer to the end of the book. Within no time at all, you will have read the entire book and not realised the amount of time taken to complete the task. This principle is so very simple, and it can be applied to every situation in your life.

Divide and conquer!

Take your time and divide all your goals into a series of smaller goals (like we just did), and your road to achievement and happiness in your life will be a very positive one.

Sing Your Way to Freedom

For centuries, music has been a major way to express feelings and emotions. You can sing to help let any trapped feelings out—feelings you might find hard to express ordinarily. Singing is a powerful way to release emotions.

Think about it: lots of songs that have been composed are expressions of love or heartbreak or other feelings held by the composer. Many composers write about things that affect them personally, and this can be seen as a form of therapy, a way of working through those emotions and resolving them.

This doesn't mean you have to go out and write songs, but there might be songs that raise your spirit and help you address how you feel about something. You can even just sing to connect with your inner artistic self … just to make yourself feel good. You can also sing about your feelings—in your own words—or sing lyrics that match how you feel (to help you release your emotions).

It you are feeling down, write out how you feel as part of that process of working through those emotions. After you have written every emotion down, find a song with a happy or neutral meaning and sing along with it. This will help you let go and feel better. The point isn't to find a song that makes you feel more down; the point is to find a song that gives you the hope and positive burst of energy you need to help address that negative feeling. You should find a song that gives you joy and hope.

I find that a good song with an uplifting tempo—usually with very good bass—takes me to another plane where my spirit can be lifted. There, negative feelings evaporate.

The aim is to really feel your song and the joy of singing it. You can even dance or move to it. Let yourself go and enjoy the moment. If you can, turn the music's volume up as high as is reasonable. Even sing and dance in front of a mirror or sing in the shower. You will feel the exhilaration and fill with life-giving energy. Remember that music is universal and fits in all places—even the bathroom!

Also, remember that singing is an art form, an expression of your true self. Most of all, remember you don't need an ear for music, and you don't need the voice of a pop star. Nobody minds what you sound like—just express yourself. It's not like you're trying to sell songs. No one needs to have an opinion. And if they do,

Gigi G.

it's just an opinion. As long as you're happy, what does it matter what others think. Just let go and be free. Enjoy the music and the freedom that comes with it. Remember …

Self-expression is the key to self-acceptance!

Self-acceptance is the key to life-long happiness!

The Classical Effect

Did you know that classical music supposedly increases a person's IQ by increasing his or her spatial intelligence or spatial reasoning skills? There have been studies showing the jump in IQ after listening to Mozart's sonatas for just ten minutes. Apparently, playing Mozart to unborn foetuses, newborns, and children can enhance brain development and intelligence. In fact, some researchers and scientists call it *the Mozart effect*. Can you believe it? There really must be something to it.

Apparently, though the primary auditory area of the brain is in the transverse superior and posterior gyri of the brain, different aspects of musical appreciation (such as pitch, rhythm, melody, timbre, and metre) are processed by other areas of the brain. These areas are found in both the right and left hemispheres of the brain. When it comes down to it, classical music seems to stimulate a lot of activity all over the brain. Apparently, the activity it stimulates all over the brain has a positive effect on people who suffer from epilepsy.[1] Now, I'm no doctor, but if that's the case, that can only be a positive thing, right?

I also heard, many years ago, that classical music calms animals and can help plants grow. I haven't tested that myself, but I do know that when I put classical music on around my kids, they are remarkably calm, settled, and focused. They really hone in on their colouring or whatever other activity they are doing at the time. That's a fact. Plus, I find it calms and settles me.

I searched the Internet for the effect of classical music on mental health one day. I found that there have been studies showing that classical music has a beneficial effect on people with low- and medium-grade depression.[2]

Apparently, this beneficial effect manifests in a number of ways. For example, dopamine production is increased naturally. And it's interesting to note that depression has been associated with low dopamine levels in some people's brains.

---

1 For example, see the following links: http://www.paulborgese.com/report_mozarteffect.html; http://suite101.com/article/psychology-of-classical-music-a53213; http://www.metaphoricalplatypus.com/ArticlePages%20Music/Music%20Epilepsy.html.
2 For example, see http://www.psmag.com/health/classical-music-an-effective-antidepressant-20226/; http://psychcentral.com/lib/2007/the-power-of-music-to-reduce-stress/all/1/; http://www.emedexpert.com/tips/music.shtml;

Apparently, people who participated in some of these studies didn't really like listening to classical music. But after a couple of months of being exposed to it, they appeared to like it more (and even asked for it to be played more often).

Classical music does produces the effects discussed so far, and it has also been shown to induce a positive mood in people, relieve anxiety, boost confidence, improve memory, increase creativity and mental alertness, and increase the release of endorphins in the body. And you know what? Endorphins have been shown to speed up healing in the body.

Clearly, it's a good thing to listen to classical music as often as you can. Of course, knowing the benefits of classical music doesn't mean you should stop taking medication for any mental health issues you might have. What I am saying is that classical music really does seem to have many positive effects on the mind and body. That is to say, this book isn't about finding one quick fix to your life. Remember there's no magic spell for happiness. Being happy is a way of life and a way of being. It's about changing the way you view yourself and the world. It's about using different techniques to help you along and make you feel good so you can maintain a happy mind and happy life.

Gigi G.

I am sharing my *own* experiences with you because I know they work. I have tried them. When I play classical music in the car or at home or at work, I feel calm, centred, relaxed, happy, uplifted, and inspired. I feel like the music has reached my soul—like a warm feeling in the chest. I feel like I can breathe easy. I feel like it's so much easier to be and feel positive when I play it because it has those effects on me. There really must be something to all this research that's out there because it actually does have those positive effects on me.

"What's this got to do with me and my happiness?" you ask.

Keeping calm, centred, positive, clear-minded, uplifted, and inspired is obviously a great state to be in. Think about it: if you expose yourself to classical music regularly (and you experience even one or two of those effects each day), your energy is naturally being put into a positive state. If those effects include the release of endorphins and dopamine into your body … even better! For that reason, why not include it in your armoury of tools used for making yourself feel good each day? You've got nothing to lose by trying. By trying, you learn something about yourself and what works for you—you only stand to gain.

You can play classical music when you wake up in the morning and while you're getting ready for the day. What better way to start the day? Or when you get home, turn it on (instead of the

TV), and listen to it while you're getting changed or making dinner. Let the music calm and centre you. This is what I do. Use it as a way to wind down from your day.

You know what? Your family can benefit from it too. My kids benefit from it! After I pick up the kids from school each day, I come home and put some classical music on for the kids so they can wind down and play while I make dinner. We listen to it together. It really seems to settle them after school each day. They've been active all day, playing and learning, and they need to wind down and relax. Otherwise, I notice they get tired and moody (and sometimes a little irrational).

If I play classical music—even if just for half an hour—by the time I serve dinner, the kids are relaxed, centred, and calm. I've also noticed that they play better together and seem to have better focus and concentration on activities such as colouring in and doing craft work, which is the type of stuff I encourage them to do while they wait for me to prepare dinner.

Another trick is to go to bed, turn it on, and let it calm you at the end of the day—even if you just listen to it with some headphones. I use headphones often because I don't want to impose my way of life on my husband. Live and let live. Though he likes classical music—especially violin solos—I respect the fact that he might not want to be listening to it as much as I do. So, headphones are a great idea.

Gigi G.

When I play classical music before going to bed, I find it can really help me sleep better. I guess it's because it has a calming and relaxing effect. And if you sleep well, you naturally feel better, don't you? I know I do. It's like a sleep bank: if you have enough good sleep each day, it builds up like money in a bank. If you don't sleep well, you get sleep deprived until you've run out of energy. If you keep taking all your money out of the bank you will fall further and further into debt—and then you have to pay interest on the money you owe. Sleep is much the same: if you keep depriving yourself, you'll be in dire need of catching up on sleep—and the interest you have to pay is the effect that it has on your health. I guess the point I'm trying to make here is that you should do whatever you can to encourage your body to sleep well each night. Otherwise, you'll have to pay an additional price to get it all back.

So what are you waiting for?

Get playing!

Let the Light in!

Have you ever noticed that some homes have their blinds or curtains drawn nearly all of the time—day and night? If you haven't, next time you are out and about in a residential suburb, take a look. You'll be amazed by how many places are closed off.

People can end up living in a closed environment, which creates an atmosphere of darkness. How can you possibly find your way in life if you keep yourself in the dark?

Are you someone who blocks out the light from coming into your home? If so, do you know what you're actually doing? You're separating yourself from the outside world and the energy of the light from the sun. You're blocking out one of the greatest miracles of nature. And when you cut yourself off from nature, you can suffer. After all, humans are part of nature.

Gigi G.

Prehistoric man—our ancestors—lived out in the open, in nature. Humans' early connection with nature and the outside world—that is, the light of the night (the moon) and the day (the sun)—dates back to when first humans appeared on this planet.

Your connection to the light is a natural part of your existence, something that you need. Think about it: your body clock actually depends on when it is light (when the sun comes up) and when it is dark (when the sun sets). Apparently, early morning sunlight helps you sleep better at night (telling your body when it's time to wake up). And didn't I just say—in the chapter before this one—that when you sleep better, you *feel* better?

So, how does the morning's sunlight help you sleep better at night?

To begin with, sunlight has always been a natural part of human existence. Our ancestors woke up with and were active in the sunlight and they slept in the dark. The cycle of sunlight and darkness regulates hormonal systems in our body and is very important in maintaining a healthy circadian rhythm. Each day you wake, your internal circadian clock needs to be reset. The best way to do that is to get early morning sunlight.

This clock actually keeps time like your watch, or better still, like a sun dial (from which the whole idea of clocks originated). So, when you expose yourself to the morning light, this appears to reset your body clock each day, so that it stays compatible with the earth's 24-hour daily rhythm.

And when it gets dark, the body is being told (by the lack of sunlight) that it's time to sleep. When you force the sunlight out of your home in the morning and during the day, you might confuse your body clock. This confusion is likely to make getting to sleep, staying asleep, and waking up very difficult.

I've actually read a number of articles that discuss the effects of light deprivation on your body. Studies reveal that when the body is deprived of natural light—especially in the morning—the body experiences dramatic changes.[3] It can affect your temperature, hormone cycle, and sleep cycle. In fact, morning light appears to be the most important factor in the running of the body's internal clock. Apparently, your body clock works best when it's exposed to sunlight between 6:00 a.m. and 8:30 a.m. The body is less responsive to the sunlight outside of this time period. In fact, it's apparently even better to go outside and expose your body to the sunlight for at least half an hour between those times.

That's why people who wake up early and go out for a walk or a jog during those times seem to have so much energy in the

---

3 For example, see http://health.howstuffworks.com/mental-health/sleep/basics/how-to-fall-asleep2.htm; http://www.scientificamerican.com/article.cfm?id=down-in-the-dark; http://www.sleepfoundation.org/article/sleep-topics/melatonin-and-sleep; http://www.medicalnewstoday.com/releases/53343.php.

morning. Their bodies are working in a natural rhythm, which means their hormone cycles are on better track. This can only be a good thing for your body, right?

You might not be able to produce the sun every morning, but you can certainly get outside and experience the natural light. This is also effective. It's much more effective than staying inside because inside light has little effect on your body clock. It's just not the same as the light nature provides. One difference is that the sun offers invaluable vitamin D for the body—inside lights don't.

And even though there are light bulbs and boxes that can simulate sunlight, there is far more value in going outside—even on an overcast day.

There are so many books and articles that talk about how natural light is also good for your mental health. Studies show that people who are deprived from direct, natural light each day can also experience depression and have a harder time coping with stress.

Why live your life in a closed box? Open up all the curtains or blinds in your home each day, and let the light in. Breathe it in! Soak it up! Feel the energy of the light—and light does have amazing energy. It powers up whole houses, so it's pretty potent stuff. Remember that it also helps plants grow. It creates life!

Think of your body parts as solar panels soaking up the energy of the light. The light can only have a positive effect on you. It will energise you and give you more life.

Do it at work too, if you can. Open up the blinds or curtains and let that light in. And if you're in an office that has no natural light, get out and soak up the sunlight. Even on an overcast day, soak up the natural light that's there and reenergise yourself.

The more you do this—at home between 6:00 a.m. and 8:30 a.m., at work, and during your free time during the day—the better you're going to feel. Your body clock will be on track, and your mood will be lifted.

And when you make this a part of your life, you'll notice the change in your mood. You'll feel balanced, rested, alive, and revitalised. You'll have energy. And when you have energy (and you're rested and balanced), you have no reason to feel physically bad. And when you feel good physically, you feel well mentally.

Happy body, happy mind!

So, light up your life and start enjoying the wonderful benefits it has to offer. It's just another ingredient in making your life a happy one.

Life's a Beach!

Imagine the sounds of the tide rolling in and out on the beach. Imagine the wind rushing through the waves. Imagine the sounds of the birds flying over the beach. All of these amazing sounds are, for me, some of the most relaxing sounds of nature. And you don't have to pay a cent to hear and enjoy them!

I listen to the sound of the water and waves and imagine all my worries being carried away. I feel so relaxed afterwards. And the wonderful thing about sitting on a beach is that you also get to benefit from the natural light. It's a double whammy! Even better is when you go for a walk on the beach. You get the benefit of the calming sound of the waves, the benefit of being outside in the natural light, and the benefit of getting your blood moving. It's even better if you can do all of this when you wake up in the morning—between 6:00 a.m. and 8:30 a.m.—when your body likes the light the most. You just can't get better than that for your body clock, your mood, your body, and your mind.

If you have a beach to go to, take your shoes off and go for a walk. If you can't walk for long, sit on the beach and enjoy the light and sounds. Close your eyes and listen to the sounds of nature around you. Feel the breeze coming off the ocean, and breathe in the crisp and clean salt air. You'll feel inspired, clear-headed, refreshed, and ready to face the day. Even if you can't get there in that early morning period, go there when you can. Connect with nature and let it carry your cares away. Let it revive you.

I honestly think that connecting with nature regularly is what our bodies want and need.

You can even sit on the beach and use the deep breathing techniques you've learned with me. Allow your mind to be calm and empty and relaxed. The sound of the tide can be so hypnotic. Just let yourself be hypnotised by it.

Nature is more powerful than anything man-made on this Earth. Whatever you do in life, try to incorporate nature into it. It's all well and good to exercise and get regular massages and meditate, but I honestly believe that when you connect with nature, the benefits can be even greater.

I sometimes feel like, when we connect to nature, we're like plugs. We plug into a socket and recharge. The Earth (nature) is the socket, full of power and energy.

Gigi G.

So, take your shoes off and walk in the sand. Let your skin connect directly with nature and the energy of the Earth. As a matter of fact, even though this chapter is about going to the beach, when you take your shoes off and walk on grass, it can have the same effect. Let your toes curl up in the grass and enjoy it.

The Earth feeds the seed from which so many things grow—there must be a natural energy in the Earth. Connect to that energy with your bare feet when you next go to the park or you're standing outside in your garden. Let your body connect with the energy of nature all around you in whatever ways you can. At the beach, walk bare foot in the sand or along the water's edge—or go for a swim. Just connect with nature somehow.

Be True to Yourself—
Dare to Follow Your Dreams

Always be true to yourself. Sit down with a pen and notepad in a quiet place. Try the beach, your backyard, or any place where you feel at peace and comfortable—any place where you feel you can relax.

Once you've done this, write everything that you have ever wanted to do in your life. This is essentially a bucket list.

Try to think back to when you were young and had dreams. When we are young, we have dreams. And have you ever noticed that the people who seem to be truly happy are doing what they wanted to do as a child?

Follow your heart. Don't worry about what others say. Be true to who you are and what you know will make you happy. Don't worry about money. If you love what you do, the money doesn't matter—and it shouldn't matter.

Gigi G.

Be like a child. Feel it in your heart and forget about trying to make sense of things. Sometimes, our decisions in life won't make sense to others, but if they make us truly happy, why do they need to make sense?

Trust your instincts; trust yourself; be true to yourself. If you're truly happy and at peace with yourself (as a result of your chosen path in life), your life will fall into place in every way.

Remember that first and foremost you deserve happiness. We *all* do. And when everyone is truly at peace with themselves (and happy), people will naturally get along. People who are at peace are accepting of others.

When following your heart and pursuing your dreams, be fearless. Remember what I said about fear: it is a negative energy that will only produce more negative energy. So, be fearless and follow your dreams with faith in your heart and faith in yourself.

If people tell you "you're too old" or "it's too late," remember this: you're never too old, and it's never too late to be happy!

The Allegory of the Frog: Run Your Own Race

A good friend once shared one of life's major lessons with me by sending me the following story called *The Allegory of the Frog*. I don't know who the author is, but it is everywhere on the Internet (with any difference between the various versions only being in a couple of words here and there).[4]

When I read it, I was blown away by the power of its message—so much so that I just have to share it with you. I honestly feel that if you follow its message like I have, you will be able to stay firm on your path to happiness and success—without fear!

---

[4] For example, see http://www.powershow.com/view/14d957-YjlkM/The_Lesson_of_Life_flash_ppt_presentation; http://jmm.aaa.net.au/articles/9989.htm; http://users.manchester.edu/Student/DBRauniyar/DeepWebPage/forward22.html; http://finance.groups.yahoo.com/group/LnT_AIT05/message/4.

Gigi G.

The story goes as follows:

"Once upon a time there was a race amongst the frogs.

The goal was to reach the top of a high tower.

Many people gathered to see and support them.

The race began.

In reality, the people probably didn't believe that it was possible that the frogs could reach the top of the tower, and all the phrases that one could hear were of this kind:

"What pain!!!

They'll never make it!"

The frogs began to resign,
except for one who kept on climbing.

The people continued:

"... What pain!!! They'll never make it! ..."

And the frogs admitted defeat, except for the frog who continued to climb.

At the end, all the frogs quit, except the one who, alone and with an enormous effort, reached the top of the tower.

The others wanted to know how he managed to do it.

One of them approached him to ask him how he had done it, to finish the race.

And discovered that he …

… was deaf!

… Never listen to people who have the bad habit of being negative … because they steal the best aspirations of your heart!

Always remind yourself of the power of the words that we hear or read.

That's why you always have to think positive.

POSITIVE!

Conclusion:

Always be deaf to someone who tells you that you can't and won't achieve your goals or make your dreams come true.

Portez-vous bien!"

Need I say more?

Seize Your Opportunities … Now!

If you have the opportunity to take on a job, go overseas, further your education at a secondary or tertiary institution, etc.—do it now! The same opportunity will never present itself to you again. Opportunities arise when the time is right for them to appear in your life.

Have you ever dreamed of becoming an actor, singer, doctor, chef, or anything else? Has that dream not been transformed into reality? Why allow your dreams to remain dreams? Persist until your dreams come true. You have your whole life to make things work out. You only have one life (on Earth) to make things happen. Do it!

Persistence is all that it takes.

The road to happiness in your life is not meant to be so easy—if it were easy, there would be no lessons in your life to learn from.

The obstacles are placed in your path so that you are able to confront the fears and problems encountered in the process of stepping over the obstacles. They also test your perseverance and persistence. Intelligence has very little to do with learning from life's lessons. Success and happiness stem from 10 per cent intelligence and 90 per cent perspiration, perseverance, and persistence. You will be a success at whatever you choose just by knowing and believing with all your heart that you will succeed. The power of your mind is incredible. Always remember that!

So, the key to your success is to set your goal and figure out what you have to do to attain it. Tell yourself that you *will* reach your goal. But always remember that lasting results don't happen overnight. Anything that manifests overnight will also disappear overnight. There must be obstacles and challenges to overcome for the results to last and be appreciated—but that is no problem at all. Always tell yourself that you have no problem with whatever you face. Say, "I have no problem with that—I can overcome that!"

For example, let us follow Jonathan down his road to happiness and success. He wanted to be a doctor since he was a young child. He studied hard at school, but he did not achieve the grades required for entry into medical school. So, he began a science degree. Each following year, he reapplied to medical school—but to no avail. After four years, he had completed his honours year with class one honours in psychology, but the school did not accept him.

By now, any other person would have given up. However, Jonathan decided to apply to all the medical schools around the country to increase his chances of acceptance. After two years of working as an assistant psychologist for a local psychiatric hospital, Jonathan was finally accepted into his first choice medical school. With his background in psychology, Jonathan became one of the country's leading psychiatrists.

Jonathan made it with persistence, but along the way he also acquired an honours degree, which led him to realise that he wanted to heal minds. His "obstacles" were constructive because they contributed to the education and development of his career. But at any one moment in Jonathan's life, he could have limited his vision to the short-term and lost all hope. Instead, he kept his mind focused on what he wanted to achieve and did not allow the obstacles to cloud his vision. The same applies to you. No matter how long it takes, everything that you do will lead you to your goal. Just keep your mind focused, and do everything that you think will lead you there. Just believe that you will succeed, and you will overcome anything in your way.

You have your dream, and now is the time to go for it. Make your dreams a reality. Only you can make them happen! You will never be happier once you have begun your journey to your ultimate goal. And try—as I said in "Slow Down and Enjoy the Journey"—to divide your main goal into a series of smaller goals.

Remember: there will be people who will put you down and criticise your dreams. Be yourself! If you want to pursue a goal so strongly, you must pursue it regardless of what others think of you. Those who criticise and gossip are extremely narrow-minded. Those people are often jealous, and they live in fear of the new and unknown. Those people don't do things out of the true love in their hearts; they are ruled by their minds. They attempt to rationalise everything around them, and they live their lives in fear of breaking the governing social mores. They are short-sighted, often considering long-term goals a waste of time. They can't be themselves and will never be able to pursue their desires. They will never be happy because they are too concerned about other people's opinions.

Avoid those people! Rise above the ignorant and be yourself! Listen to your heart alone, and always remind yourself that those people are the obstacles that you must overcome. Whoever the people are, they will never know who you truly are (or your true ability). You create your own ability by believing in yourself. Everyone has the ability. All humans are born with the same ability for greatness and happiness. The only difference between those who are not happy and those who are happy is the environment that they create for themselves—the environment within their minds. External circumstances are superficial; it is the environment we create within ourselves that will make the difference. That is the main axis of this guide; that is why you and I are travelling down this path together: to create a more positive internal environment.

Those who listen to the discouragers will lose belief in their selves and ultimately lose sight of their goals. That makes life difficult and stagnant—there is no progression towards any state of happiness.

It is so easy to believe in yourself, but people naturally hold on to old wounds and believe the worst about themselves. How sad this is! But we have worked together to rid ourselves of the desire to hold on to negative influences and emotions. We have let go, and we have the freedom from negativity to hold on to our dreams and gradually make them real.

When you have the opportunity to progress, listen to your heart and not your mind. Seize the opportunity if your heart tells you to. All positive opportunities should be seized when they present themselves—they are gifts, just as "obstacles" are good lessons. Both opportunities and obstacles will coexist. Use both to your advantage. Cherish them as though they were the most precious things in your life—they are even more valuable.

Finally, always make time to be with your positive friends or soulmates, to go out and enjoy their company. This will provide a balance between your self-indulgent activity and your ability to relate to others and consider their feelings when making your decisions. Taking everything into account, always trust that your heart will always make the right decision.

Be Your Own Best Friend

One of the most reliable ways to be happy is to be your own best friend. Learn to enjoy your own company. Listen to yourself. Be sympathetic to your own problems as you would with a friend. Offer advice to yourself as you would offer advice to a dear friend. Be kind to yourself. And most importantly, be honest with yourself.

By enjoying your own company, you will discover that you will not depend on others to make you happy. When you need to occupy your spare time and no one is around, take yourself out to lunch, dinner, or the movies. There is no written law that states that you can only go out with others to have a good time. In fact, it is worth your while to spend some quality time with yourself and get to know who you really are. Remember that you will be spending time with the *truest* friend that you will ever find—you!

You will soon understand what your needs, wants, and desires are—all of which are necessary for self-fulfilment. You will learn how to satisfy yourself at any time.

Converse with yourself in your mind. Talking to yourself does not mean that you are crazy. Discuss your obstacles, proposed solutions, plans for the day, and anything you desire to address. You can discuss anything at all. You are behaving normally—you are talking to your best friend. You are relying on yourself for your happiness. And remember, this is how it should be. Depend on yourself (and not others) for your happiness—by being your own best friend, you are simply reinforcing this.

Get up off the Lounge and Live Your Life!

When it seems that there is nothing constructive to do, avoid succumbing to the TV trap and becoming a couch potato. There is always something more constructive to do! The trick is to find out what that something is. However, the average person will decide that finding something to do requires more effort than sitting in front of the TV like a vegetable (which is what your mind will resemble if you succumb to the TV trap). The TV has a drugging effect—it numbs your mind and makes you lazy. That is why it is a trap: once you sit, it is very hard to get up! Ultimately, however, it will be far more satisfying to find something constructive to do.

One thing you can do with your spare time is grab a pen and notepad and start writing about anything that comes to your mind. Start writing a book on something that interests you (that is how I started this guide!). Write about anything, just as long as it is something satisfying to you.

This is also a great way to discover your true self. Thoughts are never ordered properly in our minds. They are jumbled together with other thoughts that don't make sense. The process of writing your thoughts on paper is a process of self-expression and clarification. You will be able to understand yourself and your beliefs more clearly. You will be able to organise your thoughts into a sensible framework and communicate them to others with confidence. The confidence you acquire from this exercise will raise your self-esteem dramatically.

Poetry is another effective way of expressing your thoughts and emotions. As mentioned above, you will sort out your feelings, fears, etc. You will unload the burden of overflowing ideas and move yourself to a level of neutrality. And remember: a neutral mind is always required in decision-making—being too emotional (or not emotional enough) will distort your perception. So, writing down your emotions will release them and effectively neutralise yourself. This will make you more satisfied with yourself.

Why not try drawing or sketching? You don't need to be able to draw like a professional. Just draw like you. Draw from your heart. You are unique, and what you produce is unique. Be proud to be unique! You can even draw a bunch of shapes—draw anything. Remember that you are expressing yourself and not aiming to please anyone else but yourself.

Find something to do that feeds your soul—that gives you peace. Meditate, walk on the beach, sit in the park and enjoy nature, sing, do Pilates or yoga, listen to music, go for a jog, do a photography course, go for a walk at sunset or sunrise, sit in a deck chair and soak up the sun, read a book, or take classes in whatever you desire. There are so many things you could do.

Find an activity that you enjoy. Anything that you do is an expression of yourself!

Remember, being active means that you are alive!

So get off that couch and live!

Change It Up!

Do you feel like you're in a rut sometimes, like your daily life needs a boost? If you answered yes, you must first ask yourself whether you're happy with yourself.

Are you happy with your life? Are you allowing yourself to follow your dreams and be happy? Are you seeing the world with positive eyes? Are you saying thank you for what you have (and for the fact that you're alive)? Are you appreciating your family? Are you appreciating and allowing yourself to experience the wonders of nature around you?

If your answer is *no* to any of those questions, there are issues you need to keep working on. You need to keep practising all the techniques we've talked about so far.

If your honest answer to all those questions is *yes*, and you still feel like you are in a rut, then you need to change things up.

Gigi G.

Change your room around. Change the office in some way if you can. Clean out things or move things about at home.

In doing this, you'll really appreciate the things you have. You might find things you forgot about and use them more.

Don't let things become stagnant and unchanged around you. You might be prone to forgetting how lucky you are if you forget about the things you do have.

Sometimes I rearrange my wardrobe and realise I have so many lovely things I bought and forgot about. I realise I don't need to go out and buy more and more all the time—I just need to remind myself that I am lucky already ... and I need to appreciate the things I have.

I find that the more often you change things around, the better you are at coping with changes in life that result from the actions of others.

So, try to change things up regularly.

Do something different, even if it's small. Keep yourself interested and stimulated. You'll really appreciate it, no matter how small it is.

Treat Yourself!

There's no reason why you can't treat yourself every now and again. And you don't have to spend money to do so.

If you're not kind to yourself, how can you ever be happy? Being kind to yourself means taking care of yourself and your needs. Treat yourself! Treat yourself like you would treat a good friend or someone you love—there's no reason why you can't do the same for yourself.

For example, when the sun is out, find a few minutes to go outside, find a park or bench, and soak it up. Relax, even if just for five minutes. There is always time.

Have a massage every now and again or go to a movie. Go for a walk or buy that piece of chocolate and enjoy it.

Gigi G.

Sometimes, I head to the park and go for a walk or sit next to the fountain so I can listen to the sound of the water falling. It's so relaxing.

Find something that makes you truly happy, relaxed, and at peace—and do it. Even if you have to put it in your diary, there is always time.

When I'm not at work, I go up to my local cafe (where my tree is), and I just sit there for about half an hour and relax. I chat to the barista and the owners and the locals, have a cup of something, and relax. This is my treat. I watch people pass by and look at the leaves moving in my beautiful tree across the road.

Another thing I do is pull out a camping chair at our house. When the weather is nice, I lie on it in my backyard and listen to the birds. Sometimes I fall asleep. It's a real treat.

Get a babysitter (if you have kids) and go out. If you're in a relationship, find time to treat yourself with some *love-time*. Reconnect and spend some alone time together. Rediscover each other and the love you have for each other. Doing this often will keep your love for each other alive.

Sometimes, I'll find the time to have a bath or read a book or listen to my music. Sometimes, if no one is home, I'll turn up the music and sing.

If you've wanted to take a course on something—such as photography or art or singing—just do it.

If there's a book you've wanted to read, but you can't seem to find the time to read it, break it down into chapters and find a few minutes each day to relax and enjoy it.

None of these things cost money. It's all about accepting and believing you're worth making the time for.

Try to treat yourself each day with *something*—no matter how small. It will make a world of difference. When you take care of your own needs every now and again, you have even more reason to be happy. Give it a try and see for yourself. You're worth it!

Get Your Own Endorphins into Gear!

When you're not feeling 100 per cent, try to avoid the instinct to run to the medicine cabinet. Try natural sunlight, connecting with nature, breathing, meditating, and self-focusing techniques that we've worked through together. Try them first to see how they go.

Get your body moving with some form of exercise—even if it's just a walk outside for half an hour. Try to get the body to work for itself and heal itself.

I also swear by apple cider vinegar. It apparently has a number of enzymes that are really good for your health. I remember someone at work telling me years ago that he swore by it. I was really sick at the time. In fact, for years after my kids were born—and especially after they started going to preschool—I

The Glass IS Full

went through a period of getting sick from everything my kids brought home. I got so sick once that I ended up in hospital with pneumonia.

During one of my particularly rough patches health-wise, a colleague mentioned apple cider vinegar. He said he had been taking it for years, and he had never been sick. It sounded too good to be true! I put his good luck down to his own biological makeup. I thought, *He's obviously one of those people who just doesn't get sick.*

Years later, a close friend of mine mentioned apple cider vinegar. He also swore by it. And then I started to think, *Wow! There really must be something to this; otherwise, why would the universe be sending me this message again?* Weeks later, I got really sick with the flu. I got on very strong antibiotics when it went into my chest. I was rotten sick.

The kids were due to go back to school after school break, and I had to go shopping to get food for their morning teas and lunches. And then I remembered the message sent to me about apple cider vinegar. So, I went to the health food section, where my colleague told me I could find it all those years ago, and I grabbed a bottle. Now, I'm no doctor—and if your doctor tells you that you need to take medicine, you should listen to him or her—but there are some situations in which you don't need prescription medication. In those cases, you could try a natural way of making yourself feel better. Instead of just grabbing the first pill you can find, try apple cider vinegar. I take two teaspoons in lukewarm water each morning and evening (after I get back from work).

That flu I had (the one I had when I went shopping) disappeared within twenty-four hours! It was amazing! I mean it. And I don't have shares in apple cider vinegar. Although, maybe I should get shares in an apple cider vinegar company because the product is so great! In fact, after five days of taking the natural remedy, I felt better than I had in years. I had energy to spare! Wow! Now, for all you parents out there with young kids, you know what an amazing thing that is—energy to spare! Unheard of. But I did (and still do) feel great.

I don't know that I can say I will never get the flu again if I keep drinking apple cider vinegar, but it's great. It just makes me realise natural remedies do work. So, if you're looking to boost your health naturally—whether its apple cider vinegar or seeing a naturopath or nutritionist or other natural therapy expert—keep an open mind. Obviously, if your body can work and stay well without having to resort to using medication, that can only be a good thing, right?

Also, always remember that part of being well is having a healthy mind. The power of the mind is unbelievable.

Becoming focused and concentrating on positive, relaxing experiences can only have a positive impact on your body and health.

I always say disease of the body and mind is simply two words put together: *dis* and *ease*. Yes, a lack of ease! But if you are positive all the time, you can remove the word *dis* and all that is left is the *ease* within you. You will have ease of body *and* mind.

But how do you take the *dis-ease* within you and turn it into *ease?* Apart from healing with natural remedies, you can try the following exercise.

Imagine yourself on a beach that is being lit by the most brilliant sunset. Imagine the water running through your toes and the wind on your face. This technique is called *imagery*. Imagine your ailment being carried away from you by the wind. Watch it fly away, and imagine it flowing out of your toes with the water. Watch it flow away. Visualise your body becoming well, and eventually you will feel better. Lighter! Like the heaviness of the illness has been lifted off you and you can breathe!

Another way of getting your own endorphins into gear is to get up and get active.

Gigi G.

Go for a walk, go dancing, take the stairs instead of the elevator. Just keep active. You don't have to work out and jog and give yourself a heart attack going to the extremes! Just lead an active life—as active as is physically reasonable for you.

Get out in the sun, and get at least ten minutes per day of that gorgeous vitamin D. Warm your soul with the sun, and it will always make you feel great and relaxed. The sun is our greatest gift. Walk for ten or fifteen minutes during lunch, and get those rays of sunshine at the same time.

Try to depend on yourself, nature, and your inner soul for your health. Use the wonders that exist in nature to keep you happy and well.

I know when I laze in the sun and soak up its rays, I actually feel good. It doesn't matter how long you spend each day doing it, just do it! I know it sounds like a cliché or some Nike ad, but honestly, just do it! There's really no sense in neglecting yourself.

I know when I was in hospital with pneumonia last year—even when I was sick as a dog in bed—I would have to go to the bathroom every now and again. When I managed to drag myself out of bed and do my business, instead of going straight back to bed, I planted myself in the armchair next to the window and soaked up the sun. I knew it would make me feel good, and I knew the rays of the sun would help my healing along.

Eventually, when I was able to harness the energy to walk for longer and farther than the few metres to the bathroom and back—when I had a pocket of energy, no matter how small that pocket was—I started getting out of bed and walking up and down the hall of the ward. And then, as that energy pocket started to get larger, I went as far as the lift once a day and took myself outside to sit in the sun and have the rays shine on me directly. I also enjoyed the fresh air. I soaked up the wonderful healing that nature had to offer me. I just did it! And so can you. All you have to do is believe that you can do it—no matter how tired or bad or sick you might feel.

Cure yourself with your own miraculous powers of faith and positivity; seize the moments you have to take care of yourself (even if just in a small way each day). And enjoy the marvellous gifts that nature has on offer. Feed yourself into a healthy body and mind, and get your own natural endorphins to work for you.

Turn down the Heat!

"What do I mean now?" you ask. I know from my own experience that overheating my body can make me feel tired and sluggish. For example, if I have a very hot shower or bath, I feel like going to sleep. I don't feel well—it's almost like I'm switched off.

I started reading about the effect of heat on the body. What did I find? Quite a bit of research, including studies and articles about the effect of heat on ageing, health, quality of sleep, and mood.[5]

---

[5] See article at http://www.normalbreathing.com/l-cold-shower.php. Also see, *Adapted cold shower as a potential treatment for depression*. Shevchuk NA. Molecular Radiobiology Section, The Department of Radiation Oncology, Virginia Commonwealth University School of Medicine, 401 College St, Richmond, VA 23298, USA. Med Hypotheses. 2008;70(5):995-1001. Epub 2007 Nov 13. Also, *[Prevention and treatment of sleep disorders through regulation] of sleeping habits]* [Article in French]. Onen SH, Onen F, Bailly D, Parquet P. Clinique du Sommeil, CHRU, Lille. Presse Med. 1994 Mar 12;23(10):485-9. Also see, *Health 20: Tap into the Healing Powers of Water to Fight Disease, Look Younger, and Feel Your Best*. Alexa Fleckenstein M.D. with Roane Weisman. 2007. McGraw-Hill Books. USA.

One of the things I read indicated that having a cold shower for a couple of minutes per day can stimulate the body's natural immune system, help people with chronic fatigue syndrome, increase people's tolerance to pain and stress, increase people's performance (mentally and physically), and help people lose weight through a process in the body called thermogenesis. For those who don't know, thermogenesis occurs when the body's metabolism increases naturally because the body is internally generating heat in response to the cold.

Another thing that really hit me was that cold showers can have a positive effect on depression. Apparently, because our bodies have so many cold receptors in our skin (as compared to the amount of warm receptors), a cold shower is like giving our bodies a mild electric shock. The shock moves along the nerve endings, which stimulates parts of the brain that are responsible for our moods.

I'm not saying that you should have a freezing shower now—if you have a heart condition, that might not be such a good idea. You don't want to put your body into shock and have a heart attack or make your body so cold that you get sick. If you have medical conditions, you really should talk to your doctor about this before you do it.

Still, there is a lot of research out there that suggests your body temperature can affect your mood. Specifically, if you overheat your body, it can lower your mood.

I turn the shower on at a lukewarm temperature and gradually cool it down towards the end. Unless it's the summer, I don't turn the hot water off altogether—but I do gradually turn the hot water down and allow the cooler water to wake me up. It really is invigorating, and I actually feel more alive and happy.

Having cooler showers or baths is worth a try. If you just make it a part of your daily routine to turn down the heat, you might find it really works for you.

Another thing I've noticed that can really affect how I feel is having too many blankets on during winter—or turning the electric blanket on and leaving it on a hot setting all night. Every time I did this in the past, I would always wake up the next morning really tired and feeling down. My body just didn't like it. So, I removed the electric blanket altogether, and now I just put one woollen blanket on the bed when it's cold.

Please note that I'm not criticising electric blanket companies at all. That's not what I'm getting at. Actually, if you do have an electric blanket, there are ways you can use it without overheating your body. For example, if you really feel the cold—and don't like jumping into a freezing bed—you could turn the blanket on low for an hour before getting into bed (and then turn it off when you get into bed). But leaving it on hot all night *might* just overheat your body and have the effect of lowering your mood and energy levels. It's just something to be mindful of. I think the best way for you to know is to try it for yourself.

It's the same principle behind having a cooler shower. The aim is not to get the body too used to being heated up all the time, it's to try to get it working by stimulating it in ways that the body is happy with. And remember: it's not about finding a quick fix. This journey with me is about learning about different ways you can stimulate happiness in yourself.

Have Faith!

I have found that, sometimes, religious organisations (or other organisations that dictate what one should believe) can plant fear in people. People sometimes fear that, if they don't believe and have faith, something bad will happen to them. But in the process, people completely forget that the most important thing to have faith in is themselves and their power. They have the power to be, the power to drive their own lives towards their destiny, and the power to be happy and live life with a happy mind in a happy place. The power is within you, but for that power to drive you towards happiness, you have to believe that you hold that power. You have to have faith in yourself and love yourself enough to want to take that power and use it to drive your life towards happiness. In short, you have to be true to yourself and faithful to yourself.

I'm not saying you can't believe in God or Buddha or Allah or any other deity, but always remember that you have the power to direct your life.

Any religion or faith that says that you have to blindly believe (and that you have no power) is taking that power away from you. You become powerless to make your life a happy one. You can never be truly happy if you don't hold the key to unlock the door that leads you to your happiness.

As controversial as this might sound, just stop to think about it for a minute. The *Bible* is a great book that tells great stories of the times before and after Christ, and it has some wonderful messages to share that give people a lot of hope. Still, it is ultimately a book written by humans who are presenting or recounting stories from their own point of view. No matter the varying strengths of people's beliefs, the simple fact remains that every human does have a different way of telling a story. There will always be different perspectives or interpretations.

I guess this is why different sects of Christianity interpret what the *Bible* says in very different ways. And where has this gotten the world? Some of the greatest wars in the world have been between different religions or different sects of the same religion. Is that what religion is about—fighting and war? No!

Gigi G.

There have been so many fights between different belief systems because people have different views. For what? In the name of religion?

If people had faith in themselves and accepted that others had different belief systems, would they still feel the need to force people to see things a certain way? Why not accept that everyone is different and entitled to his or her own views?

Know that your choices in life are just that—your choices. Can you imagine what an amazing world this would be if people accepted and embraced the fact that we are all different (and that difference makes this world an interesting place)? There would be no war, no disagreements. People would embrace individuality and every person's freedom to be himself or herself and live a happy life. We could really learn from our differences and use those lessons to help us make our own choices in life.

I know it sounds very simplistic, but that's the way it is. It is also really sad for those people who do fight because they don't accept others as they are. Our beliefs can be shared with others, and we can learn and grow as a result.

Remember: your faith and your beliefs are within you. No one can take them out of or away from you. If you believe them and have faith in who you are, why should anyone have the right to change that? And why should you try to change someone else's view if it makes that person happy.

Seriously, if we all just let each other be and allow everyone to have his or her own beliefs, there would be no reason for war. It's like I said before, the world would be *amazing!* And you know what? I really do believe it can all start with *you*—with *us*.

You just have to have faith in yourself and who you are. If you are secure and happy with who you are inside, you will have no need to change others (and no need to fight with others).

Some might say, "But I am scared that I will go to hell if I don't follow everything my religion says to follow." If you are Christian, for example, my answer for you is this: Did God preach fear and condemnation of people for being who they chose to be? No! God loves everyone, God is love, God is acceptance, and God would want you and all others to be happy—not miserable and scared of Him. He wants you to live a good and kind and positive life.

If you feel in your heart that your decisions in life are right for you and give you joy—and you are not harming anyone in the process—live without fear, accept yourself, and respect your decision to live your life to the fullest. Trusting in yourself (and in God's love for you) will lead you to happiness and success. There is no need to fear condemnation when you have God in your heart to guide you and faith in yourself to choose the right paths.

Gigi G.

The authorities in any organised religion or belief system can never be more powerful than your direct connection with the universe, your faith, and your beliefs. Just push fear aside and have faith in yourself.

Treat Others as You Want Them to Treat You!

I know it is such an old saying, but it is so true. If you treat people with cruelty and negativity, all it is going to do is come back at you (and it will probably be multiplied).

Treat people badly, and people will have no reason to treat you well in return. Why make it easy for them to treat you badly by filling them with negativity? What's the point? How miserable an existence that would be!

This is also something to think carefully about. The way you treat someone is usually a reflection of how you treat yourself inside (and the issues you have deep within you). If you criticise others freely, you are probably just as hard on yourself. You just can't be on your path of fulfilment while you allow that behaviour to continue—either towards others or yourself.

Gigi G.

You have to treat others positively and believe you deserve to be treated positively—again, not just by others, but also by yourself.

In treating others positively, learn to seek beauty in all others. Appreciate their positive aspects rather than concentrating on the negatives. Mustering the positive energy might require some effort at first, but the benefits of doing this far outweigh the negative effects created by allowing negative energy to dictate how you behave.

Part of choosing to treat others well is understanding and recognising when you are having a moment in which you're not treating someone well. If you're criticising others, you need to recognise what you're doing and say to yourself, "Stop! Do unto others as you would have them do unto you!" And then you can make the choice to stop and look for the beauty in that person. You can focus on that person's positive attributes. Each time you do this, you're changing how you view the world (and surrounding yourself with positive energy). This energy then reflects back on you, and it creates a more positive outlook within you. Eventually, you will criticise yourself less and love yourself more.

By treating others well, you will eventually be treated the same by others. Also, you will start giving yourself the same gift of being kind to yourself. Everyone wins!

Self-acceptance and acceptance of others—treating everyone with kindness—is the key to self-fulfilment and happiness.

Every Life Experience Is Positive

Some of you might find this hard to believe, but it's 100 per cent true: every life experience is positive. And, yes, I can be that certain about it.

There is a positive aspect to *every* situation in life, even if (at that moment) it appears to be quite negative. And this word *appears* is actually the key to this whole book. It is all about how you view things. Every situation can be viewed many ways. This is what makes us all different: our different points of view.

The most basic key to being happy is to have a happy view of life. You should see the good and positive in everything. As I said before, the art of being happy is learning to change that label from negative to positive until it becomes a natural thing to do.

Every time someone makes a negative remark about the weather, I always find something positive to say. For example, I often come across people stating that it is such a depressing day when it is cold or raining. I respond automatically with a comment such as, "But it is so refreshing! And it's a great excuse to stay indoors and relax." Or I say, "But what a great day to go for a walk because it's not hot." There are many ways to apply a positive spin to the situation.

When you think about it, life is full of positives and negatives. For every negative, there is an equal and opposite positive—the yin and the yang.

It takes me back to my physics classes at school. Isaac Newton said, "For every action there is an equal and opposite reaction." Who said that everything we learn at school is useless?

Take a close look at all your life experiences, and reflect on them. You will realise that, for all the experiences that you viewed as negative, there has been an equally powerful positive aspect to that situation. At the very least, one certain positive to a situation is the fact that it helps you learn something about yourself or others or a situation. Plus, all situations allow you to build on your life experience and develop your strength and character.

Gigi G.

Also, there is *always* a purpose behind every experience—no matter how negative it might seem. It is placed in your life to teach you a lesson about something and mould you into the person you are meant to become.

The art of living life and being happy is being content that life will present you with experiences that you don't need to assign negative labels to. Instead, you should label them as life lessons that will teach you and help you grow. Treat every experience as a life lesson, and look for the lesson that can be used to strengthen you. Have faith in your strength, and accept the situation with a content, open, and accepting heart. If you resist it, it will be much harder to get through. Just accept that it is a part of your great journey to becoming your fulfilled self. This can only be a positive. Don't become a victim—empower yourself, label your experiences with positive labels, and learn from them. Why? Because you can! There is nothing to stop you, but yourself!

You Are *Never* Alone!

When times seem rough and you feel isolated from the world, always remember that you are never alone. You might not be able to see it, but it's there. Whether it's someone who has died in the family who is watching over you or an angel (or spirit or God or whatever you believe in), just because you can't see it, it doesn't mean it's not there.

I often feel that my mum's father is watching me and making sure I'm safe (as a way of being there for my mum).

Have you ever noticed that, when you are feeling down or not at your best, someone says just the right thing to pick you back up? Have you ever had a question in your mind about something, and then something happens that answers that very question for you? Someone is looking out for you. When you feel down, you have to remind yourself that you are not actually alone. There is a world of angels and spirits watching out for you. You just have to have faith and trust that you will be okay.

There is a poem called "Footprints in the Sand" that has been inspiring me for years and years. Look it up on the internet. The copyright in this poem appears to be held by the estate of Mary Stevenson. Its message is powerful.

In this popular poem, a person is having a dream about walking on the beach with God. As they walk, they leave two sets of footprints in the sand behind them. These footprints represent different stages of this person's life. At one point, the person looked back and could only see one set of footprints behind him. He realised this happened at the lowest and saddest time of this person's life. Believing God had abandoned this person during this period, the person questioned God. God responded that it was during those difficult and sad times that God carried this person. The message in this poem is profound!

Every time I have felt alone in my life, I remember this poem and read it. Look it up on the internet or go to your local bookshop and ask about it. I've seen it printed on bookmarks, gift cards, and pocket-size cards. It is pretty easy to find.

Read this poem when you need inspiration and reassurance that you always have someone guiding you through the worst of times.

Always have faith that things work out the way they are supposed to. Your life will fall into the path you are meant to be on. Even if you feel things have not gone in your favour—and have not worked out exactly as you planned—always remember: you do have a path and purpose in this life.

Just follow the path and have faith all is as it should be. Whether you know what that purpose is at any given time is not something you need to worry about. When you worry, you just attract negativity to yourself. Just trust that you are not alone and you are being guided along your path with a purpose at hand.

There have been too many times to count that I have felt the power and presence of God and angels and good spirits beside me during my days and nights. They are with me, guiding me and watching over me.

I also spoke about signs. My sign is the time 1:11 (or 11:11). There have been moments in my life when I have felt down or uncertain about myself or a situation—and sure enough, I look down at my phone in that moment or my eyes catch the time on the TV, and it's 1:11 or 11:11.

Gigi G.

I once read that when you see these repeating numbers, it is a sign that everything in your life is aligned and all is as it should be. So, whenever I see this number (and it seems to appear every day), I smile to myself. I know my angels are watching over me, sending me a message to remind me that all is as it should be.

Take notice of the signs that present themselves to you when you need answers or guidance. Whoever is sending them to you is trying to tell you something: you are not alone, and all is as it should be at any given moment in your life.

Trust Yourself, Your Inner Guide, and the God within You!

By now you should know that there is no one on this Earth whom you can trust and love more than yourself. Each one of us has our own inner voice that speaks to us and offers us advice throughout our lives.

Your inner voice is your personal guide, your soul, or the God within you. I don't mean *God* in the religious sense; rather, I mean that there is great power within you in the spiritual sense.

When your inner voice speaks to you and tells you what to do, always listen to it and follow its advice. This is your intuition at work, serving and protecting you, making sure you don't forget anything important.

Gigi G.

Developing your intuition is quite easy. Just learn to trust the advice or feelings that you receive from within yourself, and follow them at all times. You know yourself better than anyone. Who better to trust than yourself?

I always find that, if I hear that niggling voice, I should pay attention to it. The most basic example I can give is when I'm at the supermarket and have a fleeting thought about milk or dishwasher liquid. When I ignore the thought, I get home and see that I needed to buy milk or dishwasher liquid. My inner voice was trying to tell me, and I chose not to listen to it. Don't doubt your inner voice. It is there to look out for you because it is connected to the spiritual world, which knows what you need.

Trust yourself and the world will be yours to enjoy!

Let It Be!

No, not the song (although the words of the well-known *Beatles* song is a good start).

Let life be.

Let others be.

Let yourself be.

When you are confronted by someone who is at odds with you, just let them be.

Getting into a tug of war with them will only cause *dis-ease* in you. And this can only make you sick and turn into an illness—a disease of some sort (because your mind and body are not at ease).

Being stubborn and insisting on getting your way all the time may seem reasonable at moments, but remind yourself that you are creating *dis-ease* within yourself by behaving this way. Plus, you are creating *dis-ease* in others—and no one wins when that happens.

The saying "agree to disagree" is apt here. Like I've said throughout the book, the key to having a happy life is letting go. Let go of all the negative feelings and accept life as it is. Accept others as they are; don't try to change people. If they're negative and don't have peace in their lives, understand that they have their own issues to deal with. Just stay away from them—they need to sort through their own issues. Just accept those people and live your life in peace.

The true essence of happiness entails being at peace—not just within yourself, but also with others and your surroundings.

When people disagree with you, you can start by offering your view. If they're open to learning from your view, that's all well and good, but the sooner you understand that you don't have to change others to be happy, the sooner you will be at peace with them and yourself.

And if you listen to their view—even if you don't agree with it—you can learn something. Even if you learn it's not your view, you've still learned there are other ways of seeing things, and that's a good thing. After all, you can only grow from experience and learning.

And if there are things that aren't so important for you to hold onto in a disagreement, let go of them. Find that common ground where you can each feel at peace. Compromise in a situation can be healthy because it forces you to assess what's important and not so important to you. Plus, it allows you to find a neutral middle ground that will enable each of you to be at peace with each other.

Remember: happiness isn't just about making yourself happy—it's also about wanting those around you to be happy. When they're happy, you're surrounded by happy energy.

For that reason, try to be in a happy place with your friends and family. Let them be, and they'll probably be more likely to let you be too. Everyone is happy!

Gather Yourself and Pull Your Life Together

Well done! You've completed your journey with me!

Now is the time to take all these tools I have given you and pull your life together with them. You're now equipped with the tools that will enable you to let go of fear and negative energies and fulfil yourself. There's no reason why you can't be happy after everything you have learned with me. You just have to believe!

You can do it!

Remember: you hold the key;
you have the power!

By applying what you have discovered on your journey with me, you'll be able to travel through life with a happy appreciation for everything it offers you along the way.

And remember to practise! The more you practise, the easier it will become. Eventually, it just becomes your way of life—how you think and how you are.

Practise is the key to your success!

I'm not going to say, "Good luck." You don't need luck. You've always been destined to be happy!

Just think about it. Fate gave you the willingness to learn. Fate gave you an open heart and mind. Fate gave you the desire to be happy. Fate led you to this journey with me.

Every moment you breathe the wonderful breath of life, remember how lucky you are to be alive. And no matter how much or how little water is in that glass, remember it is *always* full!

A Look at Gigi G.

Gigi spent her youth in England until her parents decided to move to Australia when she was seven.

Always interested in human psychology, she studied psychology at university and graduated with first-class honours before moving on to law (again, graduating with first-class honours).

In the eighteen years that followed, Gigi worked as an attorney—mainly in criminal law. With more than half her career in criminal defence, she has spent years learning about the lives and journeys of others—some of whom have found happiness. She has also searched for (and discovered) the secret to true happiness. She now shares these secrets with others in this book. She hopes to help people understand how easy it can be to be happy and how amazing the gift of life is.

Though Gigi still practises as a criminal defence attorney in Sydney, Australia, her passion is sharing the secrets to happiness with others. She hopes others will find their own paths to happiness, peace, and fulfilment. It is this joy Gigi has—generally and in helping others—that she seeks to share with the world in this book.